INSIGHT COMPACT GUIDE

LAKE DISTRICT

Compact Guide: Lake District is the ultimate quick-reference guide to this perennially popular English region. It tells you all you need to know about making the most of its attractions, from Druids' circles to wildlife parks, from the Wordsworth Museum to Beatrix Potter's House.

This is one of 130 Compact Guides produced by the editors of Insight Guides, whose books have set the standard for visual travel guides since 1970. Packed with information, arranged in easy-to-follow routes, and fully illustrated with photographs, this book not only steers you round The Lake District but also gives you fascinating insights into local life.

GW00691160

Part of the Langenscheidt Publishing Group

Insight Compact Guide: Lake District

Written by: W.R. Mitchell
Updated and designed by: Alyse Dar
Main photography by: David Beatty and Tony Halliday
Additional photography by: Alamy 23B, 26, 27T, 34, 47, 54, 68T;
Pete Bennett 7B, 19, 38, 53B, 58T, 61T; Bridgeman Art Library 82B;
Britain on View 9, 12B, 13T, 24, 25B, 37, 44, 45T, 46, 49, 56, 60, 62, 64,
66T, 68B, 72B, 73, 74B, 81, 89, 94; Corbis 31B, 63; Cumbria Picture
Library 25T; Topham Picturepoint 29T, 30, 43B, 51, 74T
Cover picture by: Peters Adams/Corbis
Picture Editor: Hilary Genin
Maps: APA Publications

Editorial Director: Brian Bell
Managing Editor: Maria Lord

CONTACTING THE EDITORS: As every effort is made to provide accurate information in this publication, we would appreciate it if readers would call our attention to any errors and omissions by contacting:
Apa Publications, PO Box 7910, London SE1 1WE, England.
Fax: (44 20) 7403 0290. e-mail: insight@apaguide.co.uk

Information has been obtained from sources believed to be reliable, but its accuracy and completeness, and the opinions based thereon, are not guaranteed.

© 2008 APA Publications GmbH & Co. Verlag KG Singapore Branch, Singapore.

First Edition 1997; Second Edition (Updated) 2007
Printed in Singapore by Insight Print Services (Pte) Ltd

Worldwide distribution enquiries:
APA Publications GmbH & Co. Verlag KG (Singapore Branch)
38 Joo Koon Road, Singapore 628990
Tel: (65) 6865-1600, Fax: (65) 6861-6438

Distributed in the UK & Ireland by:
GeoCenter International Ltd
Meridian House, Churchill Way West, Basingstoke,
Hampshire RG21 6YR
Tel: (44) 1256 817987, Fax: (44) 1256 817988

Distributed in the United States by:
Langenscheidt Publishers, Inc.
36–36 33rd Street 4th Floor, Long Island City,
New York 11106
Tel: (1 718) 784-0055, Fax: (1 718) 784-0640

www.insightguides.com

Introduction

Places

Culture

Travel Tips

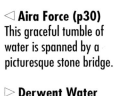

◁ **Aira Force (p30)** This graceful tumble of water is spanned by a picturesque stone bridge.

▷ **Derwent Water (p44)** One of the most beautiful of all the lakes. The lakeside views of the surrounding mountains are magnificent, and close by is the market town of Keswick.

▷ **Tarn Hows (p39)** Created by the merging of three tarns, this Lakeland icon is set in dense woodland interlaced with paths offering glorious views.

△ **Dove Cottage (p49)** This Grasmere cottage was the home of William Wordsworth and his sister Dorothy during the poet's most prolific years.

△ **Langdale (p24)** A classic mountain valley, its green floor and fellsides rising to bare rock, dominated by the outline of the Langdale Pikes, and at its head the great bulk of Bow Fell.

△ **Furness Abbey (p74)** Extending along the lovely Vale of Deadly Nightshade are the splendid red sandstone remnants of a once-thriving Cistercian community.

▽ **Beatrix Potter Sites (p40)** The famous writer lived in the pretty village of Hawkshead, and at Hilltop near Sawrey.

▷ **Castlerigg (p45)** This impressive prehistoric stone circle stands on a scenic hilltop near Keswick.

▽ **Wastwater (p67)** The most austere and spectacular of the lakes, ringed by high mountains.

Windemere (p24) The longest stretch of water in Cumbria, on its banks are the Steamboats Museum and the lively town of Bowness, from where you can take cruises on the lake.

Splendour on a Small Scale

For a million years, the Lake District was the play-ground of glaciers. A mass of ice bit deeply into an ancient landscape, plucking, gouging and smoothing to create the characteristic deep lakes and steep-sided valleys. But it isn't just the forces of nature that have conspired to make the Lake District the most striking landscape in England. Dramatic details have been added on, such as the white-washed farms on rock ledges and white-faced Herdwicks, Lakeland's own little sheep, their eyes looking as ancient as the rocks among which they forage for their herby diet. Wild daffodils flourish in the deciduous woods and also near the shore of Ullswater, where they were seen by William Wordsworth. His poem about 'dancing daffodils', which begins 'I wandered lonely as a cloud', is one of the best-known in the English language.

Opposite: moody view of the Langdales
Below: at the summit
Bottom: measure the miles

POSITION AND LANDSCAPE

An energetic person could walk across the Lake District, from Ennerdale in the west to Shap in the east, in 24 hours – a distance of about 40 miles (65km) as the crow flies. In the European context, the Lake District is tiny, yet here is a region of infinite variety. Shaped like a giant wheel, its ridges radiate from a hub of high mountains (known by the Norse term 'fells'), enfolding a host of little valleys called 'dales' and a score of big lakes. The landscape is on a comprehensible scale, not spread out as in the Scottish Highlands where mountains stand aloof from the glens and the lochs seem to go on forever. From Great End, near the heart of the district, the view north extends over Solway Firth to the blue hills of Scotland and, eastwards, to the Howgill Fells, beyond Lunesdale. The distant blue-grey smudge is the Pennines. To the west and south the sun brings a responsible gleam from the sea.

Seen from a distance, the fells appear to spring from low country – from the Cumbrian Plain in the north, the fan-shaped Eden Valley in the east and

the coastal strip of the west. Viewed from the south, the fells loom beyond a fringe of pearl-white limestone. On clear days, strollers on the 'prom' at Morecambe who look across the bay have a clear view of Black Combe, a giant brooding in isolation in the southwest of the Lake District.

On a Bank Holiday, over a quarter of a million day-trippers invade the Lake District from the conurbations of the Northeast, Yorkshire and Lancashire. Yet a short stroll away from the crowds leads to peaceful areas. Even Orrest Head, the modest knoll above Windermere, long celebrated as a vantage point, is not likely to be crowded. Half a century ago, this eminence inspired the young Alfred Wainwright (1906–91) to leave his native Lancashire textile town for Kendal, where he began his famous little handwritten guides to the Lakeland Fells.

The Lake District is a tourist's name for the heart of Cumbria. Before local government boundaries changed in 1974, the region was divided between Cumberland, Westmorland, northern Lancashire and the West Riding of Yorkshire. The Lake District National Park covers an area of 880 sq miles (2,279 sq km). This northwest corner of England is virtually an island, being washed by salt water on three sides and having an asphalt 'moat', consisting of six lanes of the M6 motorway, in the east.

One lake
The local term for lake is 'watter' or 'mere' – hence Wastwater and Windermere. Only one stretch of water has 'lake' in its title, and that is Bassenthwaite Lake, to the north of Keswick.

Ice-Age boulders at Kentmere

GEOLOGY

The geology of the area is complex. The most perceptive early student of the rocks was Jonathan Otley, of Keswick, who in 1820 published an article about 'the succession of rocks in the District of the Lakes', identifying three basic types. Knowing these simplifies the subject for the layman. Skiddaw slates, the oldest visible rocks, form the friable northern fells plus that isolated bulk of Black Combe in the southwest. They were laid down over 500 million years ago in a shallow sea. Some 50 million years later, a volcano flared. The Borrowdale volcanics of Central Lakeland were born of flame, smoke and lava-flows in a drama of landscape-formation which lasted about a million years. The Silurian slates of the Southern Lakes, composed of shales, slates, grits and flags, are (like the Skiddaw group) sedimentary. A fourth major geological element forms a narrow band of Coniston limestone between the volcanics and the Silurian slates. Clear evidence of it is to be seen by anyone who travels between the village of Coniston and Ambleside.

The appearance of the Lake District was determined 50–60 million years ago, a period of great mountain building which also thrust up the Alps and the Himalayas. In Cumbria, an immense dome was created. The radial drainage cut into the dome. During the Ice Age, ice sculpted the fells, created 'hanging' valleys, deepened and smoothed the old river valleys. The climate ameliorated and the glaciers melted some 10,000 years ago.

FORMED BY ICE

When first gouged out by ice, the lakes had affinities with one another. They have since changed at varying rates, depending on their situation and the way in which the adjacent land has been used. The least changed lake is Wastwater, in the far west, whose blueish tinge hints at near-sterility. By contrast, centuries of human settlement and intensive farming around the shallow, reed-edged

Below: yacht on Coniston Water
Bottom: Wastwater

Esthwaite Water, by Hawkshead, have enriched the water. Windermere, the largest lake, is more than 10 miles (16km) long but relatively narrow. Ullswater, which is second in size, is unlike the other lakes in that it has two bends. Its head is among the high fells, its tail in the pastoral landscape around Pooley Bridge. In addition to the big lakes, there are mountain tarns, which Lakeland artist W. Heaton Cooper (1903–95) called 'the eyes of the mountains'.

CLIMATE

Lakeland's climate is affected by the proximity of the sea and by the high fells, which form a barrier to weather fronts sweeping in from the west. The western fells are a great cloud-factory, coaxing the prevailing wind to part with its moisture. Seathwaite, in Borrowdale, tucked away among high fells near the centre of the area, has long been famous as the wettest inhabited spot in England, the rainfall being about 125 inches (3,175mm) a year.

On dull days there are usually breaks in the cloud through which sunlight streams with all the intensity of a spotlight at the theatre, bringing sections of the landscape into sharp relief. For a reliable forecast, contact the Lake District Weather Service (017687) 75757. Snow falls between December and Easter, but there is no permanent

Ambleside

cover. Pockets may linger in deep gullies until midsummer. Most valleys are low lying and a dale might remain green when flanking fells are gleaming white with snow.

FARMING STOCK

Five thousand years have elapsed since humankind made its first mark on the Lake District landscape, clearing away tracts of the old forest that extended up the hills as far as the 2,000-ft (600-m) contour. A thousand years ago, Norse settlers adjusted their lifestyle to the high hills, on which they summered their cattle and sheep. From such a hardy, independent, self-reliant stock has evolved a type of farming which has its equivalent systems in mountainous areas all over the world.

When Norman lords granted the monastic orders large tracts of the Lake District, these became a range for sheep bred from the native 'crag' sheep. Known as Herdwicks, an old English word for a monastic pasturage, the name is used to this day for the nimble little animal which has a face white as hoar-frost, a coarse fleece which is dark at first, becoming greyer with age, and four solid legs to enable it to cope with the mountainous grazing.

Farming is the basic industry of Lakeland and the one of which a visitor is most aware. The farms have stocks of sheep and a few beef cattle. Tending the sheep gives plenty of work for well-trained curs or collies, which respond to the whistles of the farmer with barks (vital here when flushing sheep from among rocks or dense areas of bracken). The Lakeland farmer is just as spirited as his forebears, who were greatly admired by William Wordsworth and his friends.

MINING AND TOURISM

The dalehead farmhouses, many of which date from the 17th century, were built of stone and slate *(see page 80)*. From the Lake District fells have come a variety of minerals, including copper, which was mined in various places, notably the

Below and bottom: sheep and shepherd

👁 Slate quarrying
Evidence of slate quarrying is to be found in many places. In the quest for good slate, quarrymen became miners. It is exciting to enter an old quarry, with pieces of slate clinking underfoot, and stand at the entrance of a man-made cave (on no account explore underground workings). In some cases, the extent of the underground works can be deduced from the draught of warm air on the face.

Below: a reminder of local mining
Bottom: walking in Buttermere

Newlands Valley. Graphite, also known as 'wadd', was hewn from underground workings near Seathwaite, at the head of Borrowdale, and became the origin of the Keswick pencil industry. Granite of various hues is quarried at Shap. The exploitation of iron ore in Eskdale led to the building of the 3-ft (0.9-m) gauge railway in 1875. In the following year, that line passed to public use. It endures today as a tourist line – the Ravenglass & Eskdale Railway (affectionately known as 'Ratty'). Slate is still quarried at the Burlington Quarry south of Coniston, at Elterwater and near the Kirkstone Pass.

Tourism is paramount in the Lakeland economy. In fact, the whole area is fast becoming a theme park. The work of Beatrix Potter (1866–1943), creator of Peter Rabbit, Jemima Puddleduck and friends, has given rise to shops dealing exclusively with her books and associated souvenirs. The National Trust, the largest landowner in the Lake District, owns Hill Top, her property at Near Sawrey, and the diminutive building at nearby Hawkshead, where her husband, William Heelis, had his solicitor's office.

WILDLIFE

The red deer is well represented in the wooded valleys of Grizedale Forest and on Claife Heights, to the west of Windermere. Red deer also occur at Thirlmere and Martindale, the last-named being a secluded valley beyond Howtown (Ullswater). Roe deer are widespread again, though deer-fencing around new plantations inhibits their movement in some areas.

The red fox is common, even though, until the recent ban on hunting with dogs, there were six active packs of foxhounds, and badgers are also found, mainly in the old deciduous woods. For years, the Lake District has been a stronghold of the red squirrel. It is still well represented in old woodland, but now the larger, more vigorous grey squirrel has gained access and is slowly extending its bounds at the expense of the smaller, daintier and now endangered red.

The Lake District is famous for its cliff-nesting species, notably the golden eagle, that for over 50 years has nested on a crag above Riggindale near Haweswater, and today, if you're lucky, a young male eagle who is still holding territory may be observed from an RSPB hide in that dale. Peregrine falcons, ravens and buzzards, which nest in fell country, are relatively common. The pied flycatcher is well suited to the mature woods. A pair of ospreys nesting west of Bassenthwaite Lake produced two chicks in 2004, the first in the English wild for over 150 years. Public vantage points are available. Canada geese are frequently seen around Grasmere, and greylag geese are locally common by Derwent Water and Coniston Water. A large colony of cliff seabirds reside at St Bees Head.

ICE AGE LEGACY

Of fish, the once-migratory char became landlocked towards the end of the Ice Age but still frequents deep water in some lakes, notably Windermere. Anglers sit in rowing boats, each with one or more long rods and groups of hooks extending from a weighted line up to 90ft (27m) deep. Of the other locally distributed fish, the schelly (a sort of freshwater herring) is associated with Ullswater. A white fish called the vendace is found in Bassenthwaite and Derwent Water.

Below: fishing in Ullswater
Bottom: gull over Windermere

HISTORICAL HIGHLIGHTS

4500BC The first hunter-fishermen appear in the Lake District.

3500BC A thriving Neolithic culture develops. Much clearing of the native forest takes place and cultivation of crops begins.

around 2500BC The first Lakeland industry is the production of axeheads from a durable volcanic tuff found high on Stickle Pike and Scafell Pike.

around 1400BC A stone circle is set on a hill now known as Castlerigg, east of Keswick. Probably the focal point for a local tribe.

1st century AD Roman domination of the fell country is maintained by roads driven through the terrain of a Celtic people (the Brigantes). The northern limit of the empire is drawn along Hardian's Wall eastwards from Carlisle.

383 Hadrian's Wall abandoned. Roman rule in the northwest crumbles with the withdrawal of troops. Local Celts, isolated by incursions of Anglo-Saxons from the east, become known as the Cymry (hence 'Cumberland').

7th century People of Anglian farming stock from Northumbria arrive in the peripheral areas of the Lake District and begin to work the most fertile ground. They leave a lasting memorial in finely-carved stone crosses.

9th–10th centuries Norse-Irish settlement from the west is the last great immigration. The newcomers, known as Vikings (from *vik*, meaning creek) follow a tradition well established in their ancestral Norway – of farms in the valleys, which they call dales, and *saeters* or summer grazings on the mountainsides, which they call fells.

1092 Following the Norman Conquest of England, William II takes Carlisle from the Scottish king and settles the area with people brought from the south.

1322 Robert the Bruce, at the head of a Scottish raiding force, visits Furness and uses the Oversands Route to attack Lancaster. A defence against repetitive Scottish raids is the pele tower, stoutly built of stone and provisioned, becoming a safe retreat for local people.

1454 First mention of a ferry across Windermere, from a point south of Bowness, in Westmorland, to the Lancashire shore.

1564 The Company of Mines Royal (a Crown monopoly) prospects for minerals (copper, lead and silver) in the Keswick area.

1618 George Preston of Holker Hall, with local help, repairs Cartmel Priory. Since the Dissolution, only the nave of this striking building had been used, the rest of the building being stripped of its roof for the value of the lead.

1643 Slate quarries are opened beside Honister Pass. Quarrymen's cottages are built at Seatoller, in Borrowdale.

1650 Ambleside is granted its charter as a market town.

1718 Lowther Village, on the vast estate of the Earls of Lonsdale near Penrith, is created as a model village for estate workers. The scheme is designed by the Adam brothers.

1750–1850 Enclosure period creates a new landscape of fields and dry-stone walls.

1799 William Wordsworth and his sister Dorothy take up residence at what is now known as Dove Cottage in Grasmere.

1835 Harriet Martineau, writer and social reformer, moves into The Knoll at Ambleside, where she lives until her death in 1876.

1845 The first steam yacht, named *Lady of the Lake*, goes into service on Lake Windermere.

1847 The railway reaches Birthwaite, which soon blossoms into a town named Windermere. Tourism flourishes.

1859 The Furness Railway is extended to Coniston. Subsequently, the company introduces a steamer service to Coniston Water with the *Gondola*. On Ullswater, a steamer service is inaugurated, from Glenridding to Pooley Bridge.

1864 Life at Keswick is transformed with the coming of the railway from Penrith.

1872 John Ruskin – writer, artist and philosopher – acquires Brantwood, on the east shore of Coniston Water. The house is greatly extended, and Ruskin lives here until his death in 1900.

1895 The National Trust is formed. Canon Rawnsley, a Lake District parson, is a founder.

1929 Manchester Waterworks begins work on the construction of a dam in Mardale, west of Shap, which will create Haweswater Reservoir.

1937 The Forestry Commission buys the 8,000-acre/3,200-hectare Grizedale Estate near Hawkshead and begins to plant trees on a massive scale.

1941 The novelist Sir Hugh Walpole dies. For many years he owned Brackenburn, on the slopes of Catbells.

1951 The Lake District is one of the 10 National Parks designated under the National Parks and Access to the Countryside Act.

1967 Donald Campbell dies when his speedboat *Bluebird* breaks up after attaining an estimated 320mph (515kph) on Coniston Water. The body of Campbell was recovered in 2001.

1974 Under local government reorganisation, the county of Cumbria incorporates Cumberland, Westmorland, Lancashire north of the Sands and a part of the old West Riding of Yorkshire.

2002 Lakeland farming and tourism recovers from a national emergency caused by foot-and- mouth disease.

2004 23 Chinese cockle pickers drown in Morecambe Bay.

2007 The bicentenary of the publication of William Wordsworth's 'Daffodils'.

ROUTE 1–3

0 _____ 5 km
0 _____ 3 miles

N

Mosedale
Greystoke Forest
Johnby
Laithes
Greystoke
Newton Reigny
Penrith
M6
Mungrisdale
Berrier Hill
Motherby
Newbiggin
Stainton
Rheged
Brougham
Scales
A66
Penruddock
Dalemain
Tirril
Threlkeld
Hutton
Dacre
Lowther Castle
Askham
Castlerigg Stone Circle
M
Keswick
A591
St John's Beck
Mosedale Beck
Trout Beck
Matterdale End
Matterdale Common
Ulcat Row
Watermillock
Pooley Bridge
Helton
Whale
Hackthorpe
Lowther
Wildlife Park
High Seat 608m
Castle Rock
Dockray
Gowbarrow Fell
A592
Barton Fell
Great Dodd 856m
Aira Force
Sandwick
Bampton
Thirlmere
Stybarrow Dodd ▲840m
Ullswater
Loadpot Hill 671m
Rosgill
Watendlath
Glenridding
Place Fell 657m
Martindale Common
Bampton Common
Borrowdale
Helvellyn 949m
Patterdale
Dale Head
Haweswater Reser.
Swindale Beck
Ralfland Forest
Stonethwaite
LAKE
DISTRICT
Bridgend
High Raise 803m
Striding Edge
Hartsop
Hayeswater
Mardale Common
Seat Robert
Ullscarf 726m
Wythburn Fells
Wythburn
Fairfield ▲873m
Brothers Water
High Street ▲829m
High Raise 762m
Dunmail Raise
C U M B
Nan Bield Pass
Gatescarth Pass
Shap Fells
NATIONAL
A591
Middle Dodd 776m
R I A
Great Yarlside
Langdale Pikes
Dove Cottage M
Grasmere
Rydal Mount
Kirkstone Pass
A592
Ill Bell 755m
Harter Fell 778m Kentmere Reser.
PARK
Borrow Beck
Sadgill
Pike of Blisco 702m
Blea Tarn
Elterwater
Rydal Water
Clappersgate
Ambleside
Kentmere
Kent
Long Sleddale
Wrynose Pass
Brathay
Skelwith Bridge
Roman Fort
Longhrigg
Troutbeck
Applethwaite Common
Staveley Head Fell
Forest Hall
Furness Fell
Tarn Hows
Hawkshead Courthouse
High Wray
Townend
Holehird
National Park Visitor Centre
Troutbeck Bridge
Garnett Bridge
The Old Man of Coniston ▲803m
Steam Yacht Gondola
Hawkshead
Esthwaite Water
Hill Top
Windermere
Windermere
Staveley
A6
Watchgate
Coniston
A593
Brantwood
Brantwood
Near Sawrey
Bowness-on-Windermere
Burneside
Grizedale
Mitchelland
Crook
GRIZEDALE
Blackwell
A5074
Winster
Kendal
Blawith Fells 255m
FOREST PARK
Satterthwaite
Crosthwaite
Grigghall
Abbot Hall Art Gallery M
A591
Oxenholme
Force
Thwaite Head
Bowland Bridge
Row
Low
Brigsteer
Natland
Woodland Fell
Rusland
Lyth Valley
Sizergh
Oxen Park
Lakeside
Cartmel Fell
Howe
Pool Bank
Lowick
Colton
Newby Bridge
Staveley-in-Cartmel
Witherslack Hall
Levens
Sedgwick
Stainton
Spark Bridge
Backbarrow
Witherslack
Hincaster
Greenodd
Haverthwaite
Ayside
High Newton
Town End
Leasgill
Heversham
Woodhouse
Broughton Beck
Field Broughton
Milnthorpe
M6

1: To the Shores of Windermere

Levens and Sizergh – Kendal – Kentmere – Windermere – Bowness – Lyth Valley (37 miles/60km)

Map on page 18

Southeast Lakeland lacks the drama of upjutting and craggy volcanic rocks, such as may be seen in Central Lakeland. But, tucked away among its quieter hills are fascinating places. In the limestone country a few miles south of Kendal are Levens and Sizergh, two contrasting stately homes. Kendal, the 'auld grey town', another reference to limestone, is now bypassed, which makes the place marginally quieter than it was. Real tranquillity can be found in picturesque Kentmere. This valley is a cul-de-sac for motorists, but the hill-walker strides briskly on.

The destination on this route is Windermere, England's largest lake. The old steamers (now running on diesel) ply the lake and take the visitor to within sight of the rock turrets of the Langdale Pikes. Bowness Bay, a bustling place which the writer Arthur Ransome referred to as Rio, has a fascinating waterfront and the country's finest collection of steamboats. The return to Kendal is through the Lyth Valley, back in limestone country. The limestone gives a special flavour to the fruit of a profusion of damson trees, which are white with blossom in May and bough-bent by fruit in September and October.

Preceding pages: Loweswater
Below: Cumbrian post

LEVENS HALL

Having left the M6 at Junction 36 for Kendal, follow the A591 as far as the intersection with the A6 then turn left for ★ **Levens Hall** (April–mid-Oct, Sun–Thurs; hall noon–5pm; gardens 10am–5pm). This unusually proportioned house, home of the long-established Bagot family, proclaims its great age. A 13th-century pele tower *(see page 79)* was incorporated into an Elizabethan mansion by the Bellinghams. Then a kinsman took over Levens: Colonel Graham, whose great contribution to the house was the fine furnishings, Jacobean style, set off by panelling, plasterwork and a range of paintings. Graham also commissioned the gardens, which are notable for their topiary, designed by Monsieur Beaumont, the King's gardener, in 1690.

The original plans have survived, so the garden is true to the original concept. Light refreshments are served in the house. Just across the road from Levens Hall is parkland, adorned by venerable trees and open at all times – there are public footpaths. To be seen in the park are dark-phase fallow deer and black-and-white Bagot goats.

Below and Bottom: Levens Hall pele tower and topiary

Sizergh

Head back on the A6 until you reach the sign for ★ **Sizergh Castle** (April–Oct, Sun–Thurs 1.30–5.30pm), a Norse name meaning 'Sigrid's shieling'. Once the home of the Stricklands, Sizergh is now owned by the National Trust. As at Levens, the core of the building is a 13th-century pele tower, and this was extended into a fine Elizabethan house. Of special note are the Elizabethan carved overmantels. Also on view are English and French furniture, and Stuart-period portraits.

The garden, largely 18th-century in character, has a large rockery (noted for its hardy ferns) and two small lakes. The grassland is kept in a natural state, and in spring and summer it is bright with bulbs and limestone-loving flowers, including orchids.

Kendal

Kendal (clearly signposted from the bypass) lies just outside the Lake District National Park. The wool trade transformed the town and led to the construction in the 18th century of many small yards, some good examples of which remain and are worth exploring.

Notice in Stricklandgate an estate agent's shop with a protruding sign, a hog with bristles, originally made when the premises were used by a maker of brushes. The main clock is at the **Town**

Hall, rebuilt on a grand scale in 1825. On market days, Wednesday and Saturday, the country-folk would jostle with those of the town at stalls in the **Market Place**.

Today, Kendal is celebrated outside the Lake District as the home of Mint Cake, a slabby, mint-flavoured confection widely used by walkers and climbers but available to all. Park the car (there is a multi-storey car park) and follow one of the Discover Kendal trails, details of which are available from the Tourist Information Centre.

Star Attraction
● **Abbot Hall Art Gallery**

RIVERSIDE AND MUSEUMS

A broad riverside path west of the River Kent is traffic-free and leads to ★★ **Abbot Hall Art Gallery** and **Museum of Lakeland Life** (April–Oct, Mon–Sat 10.30am–5pm, till 4pm Oct–Mar). Here is an outstanding collection of fine art, shown on a rotation basis, including works by Picasso, Matisse, and portrait painter George Romney (1734–1802). There are also interesting historical displays, with two rooms devoted to the life and work of Arthur Ransome (1884–1967), the author of *Swallows and Amazons*. Visit also the ★ **Kendal Museum** (Thurs–Sat, noon–5pm), near the railway station. This museum has imaginative displays relating to archaeology and natural history.

Fields of Kendal Green
This is a town with its sleeves rolled up and its motto – *Pannus mihi pani*, 'wool is my bread' – reflects its former importance. Camden, writing in 1582, saw the 'tenter fields' where cloth was stretched out to dry after being dyed, and compared the sight with 'vine orchards in Spain'. Kendal Green was the most famous local colour, achieved by mixing woad (blue) with dyer's yellow broom. One of the customers was Robin Hood.

Kendal's celebrated Mint Cake

Map on page 18

There is a section comprising items associated with Alfred Wainwright, the celebrated guide-book compiler.

Shopping and Sightseeing

By Abbot Hall is the ★ **Church of the Holy Trinity**, which began to take shape in the 12th century and continued until it reached a grand scale through the generosity shown by the wool merchants who endowed it. One of the aisles is named after the Flemish weavers who were brought in to help the town become prosperous. The first impression on entering the building is one of vast size – the church is 103-ft (31-m) wide. Displayed on the north wall is a helmet, said to have belonged to 'Robin the Devil', the nickname of Colonel Huddleston Philipson who rode his horse into church during divine service. He was seeking but did not find Colonel Briggs, one of his Cromwellian adversaries.

K Village Outlet Centre (Mon–Fri 9.30am–6pm, Sat 9am–6pm, Sun 10.30am–4.30pm, Bank Hol 9.30am–6pm; reduced hours in winter) has a handy riverside location at the south of the town and offers for sale a wide range of home and garden products, fashion, sportswear and footwear at large discounts. Diversions include a restaurant, a picnic area and children's play area. The **Brewery Arts Centre**, in Highgate, is a lively multi-arts complex, incorporating theatre, cinema, live music, as well as the Green Room Restaurant, with garden patio and two bars. **Kendal Leisure Centre** (daily 7.45am–10.15pm) is a large modern building, serving South Lakeland. There is no charge for the use of the car park, and facilities within the building include swimming. Many celebrities have appeared in productions at the theatre.

Croppers of Burneside

In Burneside you can visit the shop associated with the paper-making concern of James Cropper, whose enterprise grew lustily in the second half of the 19th century and, by keeping up to date with modern means of production, has celebrated its centenary. James himself died in 1900, but the family connection remains. Another Burneside Cropper of note was Margaret, a poet and hymn-writer.

Burneside Hall

Burneside

On leaving Kendal, avoid using the often congested A591 north by taking a right turn onto the B5284, just beyond the old County Hall, for

Burneside, where the water of the Kent has been used as power for mills since corn was first ground here in 1283. The most venerable building in Burneside is the Hall, now a farmhouse, where lived the 'Burnesheads'. Like many another old building in this part of Cumbria, the house was an addition to a pele tower (here somewhat ruined).

KENTMERE

Cross a bridge over the **River Kent** and continue on a minor road by Hagg Foot and Spring Foot. The woodland between the road and river is brightened in spring by clusters of small wild daffodils. **Dorothy Farrer's Spring Wood**, a mile east of Staveley, is a nature reserve of the Cumbrian Wildlife Trust (non-members need a permit), where in more open areas the springtime flora includes bluebell, dog's mercury, lords-and-ladies and early purple orchid. Cross another bridge, about a quarter of a mile from Staveley, and turn right to follow the road into secluded ★ **Kentmere**. The road meanders amiably through a knobbly and well-wooded landscape. The glint of water indicates what remains of **Kentmere Tarn**, which shrank considerably when the valley was drained to reclaim land for agriculture. Parking in Kentmere is carefully regulated. There is usually space (for a fee) in a small field near the

Below: house at Hagg Foot
Bottom: village church in Kentmere valley

Map on page 18

bridge. The road ends about a mile north of the village, beyond which is a rough track leading to Nan Bield Pass, which connects Kentmere with the Haweswater valley.

ST CUTHBERT'S CHURCH

St Cuthbert's Church sits on a ledge high above the valley and presides over a scattering of houses and farms. Amble along the little lanes and cross the tiny bridges, surrounded by an astonishing stonescape. Keep bearing right, crossing a bridge over the River Kent and returning to the village on a lane between high walls.

There are views up the valley of fells in the Borrowdale volcanic zone, including Yoke and Mardale Ill Bell, beyond which is High Street. They are part of a horseshoe of high ridges which appeal to the tougher fell walkers. A much more gentle stroll from the church is to Kentmere Hall, another building which developed from a simple pele tower, a sanctuary for the favoured local people. The 15th-century hall, which served as a farmhouse for a long time, can be seen from the road.

Transported by glaciers
Enormous boulders lie in the fields around St Cuthbert's Church, borne to their resting places by glacial ice. Others have been incorporated in drystone walls, demonstrating as well as anywhere the drystone waller's special skills.

WINDERMERE AND BOWNESS

Return to Staveley and the A591, turning right for **Windermere**, which before the arrival of the rail-

Steamer on Lake Windermere

way in 1847 was the hamlet of Birthwaite, situated a mile from the lake anciently known as Vinard's Mere. A railway service still operates, though part of the station site is now occupied by a supermarket, with a café. There is also a large retail outlet of **Lakeland Plastics**, with a café and car park.

Windermere is very much a Victorian town, with a variety of shops. Continue down Lake Road to Bowness and park in one of the large parking areas by Bowness Bay. **Bowness-on-Windermere** is a town around which to saunter. The promenade at **Bowness Bay** has a gala atmosphere as boats come and go at the various piers, waves lap against shingle, gulls squawk and the majority of swans seem to spend most of the day out of the water, waddling about begging for food. The 'steamers' – *Swan*, *Teal* and *Tern* – are operated by Windermere Lake Cruises. Their service runs between Lakeside, Bowness and Waterhead (for Ambleside). Windermere Lake Cruises also organises winter sailings. 'Freedom' day tickets are available.

Soaking Up the Atmosphere

The most historic building, ★ **St Martin's Church**, has an east window which consists of 15th-century glass said to have been brought from Cartmel Priory *(see page 77)*. **Belsfield**, at one time the home of the Furness industrialist H.W. Schneider, is now a hotel. Schneider's iron-hulled boat, *Esperance*, is part of the Windermere Steamboat Collection. Formerly displayed at Windermere Steamboats and Museum, which closed in 2006, *Esperance* and other vintage Lakeland craft from the acclaimed collection will be housed in a new lakeshore complex for which plans are underway. The collection includes Beatrix Potter's rowing boat and *Dolly*, which is the world's oldest mechanically powered boat – it was launched in 1850, sank nine years later, and was recovered in 1962.

Occupying a central position at Bowness is **The World of Beatrix Potter** (closed Christmas Day and the last three weeks in January). An exhibi-

Cross Lakes Experience
Plan to leave your car behind for a day. The flexible Cross Lakes Experience ticket allows you to explore the Windermere-Bowness-Hawkshead-Coniston area by boat and bus with options for walking and cycling between certain points. There is a bus service from Windermere Station to Bowness Pier 3 from where boats depart. Telephone 015394 45161 or visit www.lake-district.gov.uk/map for further details.

Below: chatting and strolling in Bowness-on-Windermere
Bottom: Mrs Tiggy-winkle at The World of Beatrix Potter

Map on page 18

tion creates the atmosphere of walking through her books and meeting the characters. There is a Potter-themed tearoom with tables indoors and on the garden terrace.

Blackwell

From Bowness, follow the A5074 (which begins opposite the church) to the signposted turning for ★ **Blackwell** (mid-Feb–Dec, 10.30am–5pm, reduced hours in winter), the Arts and Crafts house designed by M.H. Baillie Scott for a wealthy Manchester brewery owner. Built between 1897 and 1900, Baillie Scott's experiment in light, space and texture has been sympathetically renovated.

Lyth Valley

Return to the A5074 now and proceed through the **Lyth Valley**, *lyth* being a Norse word referring to the long slope leading up to the limestone plateau of Whitbarrow. Although it has an A classification, the road has an easygoing manner and offers long views over Windermere.

A few minutes' further south, in a knobbly countryside of little fields and scattered homes, lies **Winster**, with a much-photographed, white-walled post office in a house dated 1600. Its environs are a riot of flowers in summer. Just beyond Winster, the name of a roadside hotel, **Damson Dene**, draws attention to a famous product of the Lyth Valley, the damsons, which have a nutty flavour. Ripe by September, some are eaten immediately, others are preserved as jam – and yet more go to make gin.

In May it's worth driving down the valley and back again to see the glory of damson blossom, which in a good year gives an impression of a light fall of snow.

Near Damson Dene, an unclassified road on the right leads to Bowland Bridge. Continue up the hill beyond the bridge, where a signpost indicating ★ **Cartmel Fell Church** is seen. In summer, the church and its yard are tucked away behind a screen

High Fells viewpoint
For a magnificent view of Lake Windermere, head for Biskey Howe, which is reached by following the steep Helm Road (just off Queen's Square in Bowness) and then going left for a few yards/metres. In clear weather, many of the high fells are visible from this viewpoint.

The main hall at Blackwell

of leaves. The building dates back to the early 16th century, when it was a chapel-of-ease in the parish of Cartmel, a village about 7 miles (11km) away. The furnishings include a three-decker pulpit and fascinating pews, one (for Cowmire Hall) seemingly fashioned from the old chancel screen.

Return to **Damson Dene** and take the road that goes as straight as an arrow to **Crosthwaite** ('clearing where a cross was raised') on the northern side of the Lyth Valley. There is no Lyth Beck, just two little rivers, one called Pool and the other Gilpin. This part of the Lake District is in delightful contrast with the austere fell country. There are relatively small fields, lots of trees and some hedges as well as walls.

Below: the view from Scout Scar
Bottom: Bowland Bridge

SCOUT SCAR

Follow the signs for Kendal on an unclassified but well-surfaced road. The road climbs over **Scout Scar**, the name *Scout* coming from the Norse *skuti*, meaning a steep cliff. The name is accurate: Scout Scar has a fearsome series of limestone crags and an almost level ridge walk extending south for well over a mile. Park the car in the car park at the summit of the road, cross the road and follow a path along part of Scout Scar to a **mountain indicator** nicknamed 'The Mushroom' because of its distinctive shaped roof.

The road leads from Scout Scar back to Kendal.

Map on page 18

2: Ullswater and Kirkstone Pass

Penrith – Ullswater – Glenridding – Patterdale – Hartsop – Kirkstone Pass – Troutbeck – Ambleside – Dacre – Penrith (52 miles / 84km)

Ullswater stretches from craggy volcanic fells to an altogether softer landscape resting on friable Skiddaw slate. The fells assembled around the upper reach appear to leap straight from the water, like mountains from a Norwegian fjord. There was once a passion, on the part of those with taste and leisure, to shatter the silence and listen to the echoes. The Duke of Portland mounted some brass guns on a boat. One who heard about it suggested that the Duke might 'let a few French-horns and clarionets be introduced.' Unlike other lakes, Ullswater has two pronounced bends, giving it a shape rather like a dog's leg. The name is Norse, meaning Ulfr's lake – although which Ulfr gave his name to the lake is hard to say, as the name was common among the Norse settlers.

Ullswater schelly
The schelly, only found in Ullswater at the deepest part, are threatened with extinction and are a protected fish. If caught accidentally, they must be carefully returned.

RUGGED HILLS

Kirkstone Pass takes its name from a large pointed rock, said to resemble a kirk. The road is the A592. It crests at 1,489ft (454m), but is kept open throughout the winter when some other high

Ullswater

Lakeland passes are left to the snow-dogs. Early tourists who wrote about their experiences on Kirkstone Pass chilled their hearers. Celia Fiennes (1698) was 'walled on both sides by those inaccessible high rocky barren hills which hang over one's head in some places and appear very terrible.'

On the route described here, Kirkstone is crossed twice, the second time being from south to north, when the views across the fells are most dramatic.

PENRITH

Lying just off the M6, **Penrith** has about it a ruddy tinge from red sandstone. The town name relates to a crossing point of the Eamont, the outflow of Ullswater. The market tradition which began in the 13th century had a modern expression in the recent creation of an auction mart near the big M6 roundabout. The 14th-century **Castle** is a picturesque stump, with grassed-over moat, in a park near the railway station. No charge is made for a visit.

Georgian ★ **St Andrew's Church** dates from 1722. In the churchyard are upreared stones known as the **Giant's Grave** and associated in legend with an ancient Cumbrian king.

The Romans had an important fort at Brougham, a mile or so down the road towards Appleby. Brougham Castle (English Heritage) is the former home of the Clifford family. Just off the A6 south of Penrith is the Estate of the Lowthers, Earls of Lonsdale, whose family name was bestowed on the River Lowther.

Rheged – The Village in the Hill (daily 10am–5.30pm) reached from the M6 at Junction 40, using the Keswick Road, is named after Cumbria's Celtic Kingdom. Europe's largest grass-covered building contains a cinema, exhibitions, and shops and several pricey places to eat. The **Lakeland Bird of Prey Centre** (April–Oct, daily) has a diverse collection of hawks, eagles, owls and falcons and offers daily falconry displays (noon, 2pm and 4pm).

Below: Rheghed Visitor Centre
Bottom: Lakeland Bird of Prey Centre

Map on page 18

Dalemain

Leave town by the Keswick road (A66) and at a roundabout bear left (A592) for Pooley Bridge and Ullswater. The mansion seen to the right of the road, 3 miles (5km) from Penrith, is **Dalemain** (Easter–mid-Oct, Wed–Sun and Thurs 11am–4pm), home of the Hasell family since 1679. Dalemain is really three houses in one: it is Georgian in outward appearance, the facade hides an Elizabethan house, and at the core of the building is a Norman pele tower. A herd of fallow deer occupies a walled park behind the house.

Where the A592 comes in sight of the lake, bear left for **Pooley Bridge**, which has a backdrop of a wooded hill called **Dunmallet** (*dun* indicating a hill fort). A fast-flowing river, the Eamont, is a tributary of the Eden (car park by the river, near the narrow road bridge).

Fragrant walkways
Over 100 old-fashioned roses and numerous 18th-century named-variety apple trees perfume the gardens at Dalemain. Apple soup is one of the seasonal dishes served in the tearoom, which is set in the mansion's medieval hall.

Garden statue at Dalemain

Ullswater

Ullswater, not quite 8 miles (13km) long, has a sinuous appearance and a setting which gets progressively grander with the passing miles. It was on the shore of this great lake that William and Dorothy Wordsworth saw the 'dancing' daffodils. Dorothy Wordsworth jotted in her journal her impressions of 'a few daffodils' close to the waterside. She placed the spot 'beyond Gowbarrow Park' (presumably to the south of the junction between the A592 and A5091 to Dockray). Wrote Dorothy in 1802: 'They grew among the mossy stones about and about them; some rested their heads upon these stones as on a pillow for weariness; and the rest tossed and reeled and danced, and seemed as if they verily laughed with the wind…' Between 1804 and 1807, Wordsworth adapted her prose as a poem, beginning: 'I wandered lonely as a cloud...'

★★ **Aira Force** belongs to the National Trust, which has provided adequate car-parking facilities. The falls are seen after following a good path that climbs steadily for about a quarter of a mile (0.5km). The slender waterfall tumbles a total of 60ft (18m) in a gorge flanked by trees.

A small stone bridge spans the gorge. The Force has occasionally frozen, becoming an impressive icicle. **Gowbarrow Fell** (a former deer park) is a place on which to wander, at relatively low elevation, with grand views of Ullswater. Walk on to Gowbarrow by going northwards from the Aira Force car park, then bearing left to the ruins of a shooting lodge. After reaching the summit, continue to the valley of Aira Beck and return via the popular footpath used by visitors to the falls.

Star Attraction
● Aira Force

Below: Aira Force
Bottom: Helvellyn

Glenridding is said to mean 'glen overgrown with bracken'. Goldrill Beck from Brothers Water is the main feeder. Since the **Greenside Lead Mines** closed in 1962, after being worked for three centuries, the area has been landscaped. The village is almost entirely touristy, but attractive. A bridleway links up with a footpath extending to the summit of **Helvellyn** (3,118ft/950m), a mysterious hill. The name is possibly Celtic, but no convincing derivation has been advanced. Others make a climb direct from Glenridding and (choosing dry, calm conditions) negotiate the fearsome **Striding Edge**.

LADIES OF THE LAKE

★ **Ullswater Steamers** operates daily services (open all year, weather permitting; closed Christmas Eve and Christmas Day) in the boats *Raven,*

Map on page 18

Lady of the Lake, *Lady Wakefield*, and the smaller vessel, *Lady Dorothy*. The 'Steamers' sail from Glenridding, Howtown and Pooley Bridge, offering one- and two-hour cruises. One-way sailings are ideal for walkers exploring the valley.

Patterdale, between Glenridding and Brothers Water, is named after St Patrick. A local tradition has it that the saint took refuge here after being shipwrecked on Duddon Sands in AD540. The church is dedicated to the saint, who is said to have preached in this area and baptised converts at a lakeside spring.

HARTSOP

Dovedale, a tributary valley, ends on the shores of **Brothers Water**, an expanse of water under half a mile (0.8-km) long and a quarter of a mile (0.4-km) wide. The name was formerly Broad Water, but romance invests it with the sad tale of two brothers who drowned when ice broke beneath them. This area is owned by the National Trust. From a car park near the outflow of the lake there is a pleasant walk to the vicinity of ⋆ **Hartsop Hall**, a massive 15th-century structure. On the opposite side of the main road, the village of ⋆⋆ **Hartsop**, with 17th-century buildings, reclines in a motoring cul-de-sac. A track continues into the Hayeswater Valley, under the massive bulk of High Street. The place name

Below: Townend
Bottom: Hartsop village

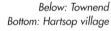

Hartsop means 'valley of the hart', which is apt, for red deer from the 'forest' at Martindale are seen in the area. Hartsop has a workaday farm and some dwellings with 'spinning galleries', where (it is said) spinsters spun wool from the fell sheep.

Star Attractions
- **Hartsop**
- **Townend**
- **Holehird**

KIRKSTONE PASS

Kirkstone Pass is something special in a region rich in superlatives, though the crossing can be dreary in wet or misty weather. Near the summit is **Kirkstone Pass Inn**, which has evolved from a late 15th-century building. The thick-walled, heavy roofed building looks across to the face of Red Screes. There are easier ways than the Screes for anyone wishing to gain the 2,541-ft (775-m) summit of Middle Dodd. A path from the car park leads northwards for about half a mile to where 'the kirk stone', a 10-ft/3-m boulder stands on an eminence near the road.

> **Troutbeck Church**
> The large east window of Troutbeck Church was the work of a famous trio – Edward Burne-Jones, William Morris and Ford Maddox Brown. Morris was assisted by the others when they were having a Lake District fishing holiday. Ann Macbeth, who lived locally from 1921 until 1948, adorned the building with splendid tapestries.

TROUTBECK

On the way down to Windermere, make a diversion to **Troutbeck** village, with its fascinating assembly of 17th- and 18th-century buildings. The **Mortal Man** is an inn with a sign relating to an especially strong ale: *Thou mortal man, who liv'st by bread, /What is it makes thy nose so red? /Thou silly fool, that look'st so pale, /'Tis drinking Sally Birkett's ale.*

    Several roadside wells in Troutbeck are dedicated to saints. At the southern end of the village, and appropriately named ★★**Townend**, is a superb house, cared for by the National Trust (April–Oct, Wed–Sun 1–5pm or dusk if earlier). Townend was built by a yeoman in the 17th century and lived in by the Browne family, generations of whom furnished it with an array of exquisitely carved wooden furnishings and a collection of over 1,500 books. The existence of this lovingly preserved library is historically significant.

    Continue on the A592 towards Windermere, but look out for a sign relating to ★★**Holehird**. The mansion, now a Leonard Cheshire home pro-

Below: Troutbeck Church window

Map on page 18

viding care for people with disabilities, is not open to the public, but the gardens are maintained by the Lakeland Horticultural Society and can be viewed (April–Oct, 10am–5pm). They include a wide range of alpine and rockery plants, and a tree, Davidia, which produces handkerchief-like bracts in spring.

At the roundabout on the A591, go right for Ambleside and after passing through **Troutbeck Bridge** and along a stretch of road flanked by mature beeches, look out for a sign to the left for the ★★**National Park Centre, Brockhole** (Feb–Oct, daily 10am–5pm). The grounds (open all year), with their splendid views of Windermere and the Langdale Pikes, were designed by Thomas Mawson in 1898. A large pay-and-display car park is handy for the main buildings; access and assistance are available for disabled visitors. The formal gardens include shrub roses, herbaceous borders, scented and kitchen gardens, and a wildflower meadow. Brockhole offers audio-visual presentations, themed trails, boat cruises, drystone walling, and exhibits. There is a gift shop and a café with terrace.

> **Landscape language**
> Place names record the history and heritage of the county. Celtic, Norse, Irish and Norman have all been great influences. Old English 'pike', as in Langdale Pikes, (from *pic*) means a peak or sharp summit. Stickle from *sticele* or *stikill*, a steep place.

Tea on the terrace at Brockhole

AMBLESIDE

Ambleside has been described as the hub of the wheel of beauty. Roads radiate into the central valleys, and Windermere Lake Cruises operates from Lakeside, a mile away. A trolley service runs between the pier and the White Lion Hotel in the town centre (Easter–Oct daily, Nov–Easter Sat). Ambleside is a mainly Victorian town of splendid slate buildings constructed by craftsmen. The spired Victorian **church** contains a mural relating to a local custom, the Rushbearing, which takes place in July *(see page 49)*. The diminutive **Bridge House**, beside Rydal Road, spans the beck and is an information centre run by the National Trust. Close by is the **glass-blowing workshop** of Adrian Sankey, and higher up the beck is an old **corn mill** complete with waterwheel. Market day is Wednesday, when stalls are set up in King Street. **Ambleside Museum and**

Armitt Library (museum daily all year 10am–5pm, except Christmas; library Tues and Fri only 10am–4.30pm) presents the history of Ambleside through various exhibits and activities. The entertaining **Homes of Football** gallery (daily 10am–5pm) displays a selection of images by sports photographer Stuart Clarke.

Star Attraction
● **National Park Centre,
Brockhole**

THE STRUGGLE

From Ambleside head back to the Kirkstone Pass, via the steep road known appropriately as **The Struggle**, which starts opposite the large car park on Rydal Road and crawls up a steep gradient to Kirkstone Pass Inn on the A592. Look out for the views northward from the pass, which are magnificent. Soaring fellsides, littered with boulders, frame a picture of Brothers Water and the high fells east of Patterdale.

Motor on through Glenridding to a point just beyond Watermillock and turn left on an unclassified road, following the signs to **Wreay** and **Dacre**. Dacre is something special, being genuine, with no tourist ploys, and having a history which boggles the mind. The church is believed to have been the site of Dacore, a monastery mentioned in Anglian times by the Venerable Bede, who relates that a young man whose eyelid was swelling at a fearful rate had it touched with a lock of the hair of St Cuthbert and within a few hours

Ambleside: Bridge House

Map on page 18

had been cured. **Dacre Castle** (not open to the public) dates from the mid-14th century. It became the property of the Hasell family in 1723 and was then restored. A further restoration took place in the 1960s, when it became the home of Bunty Kinsman. Her amusing account of life at Dacre Castle was published in 1971 under the title *Pawn Takes Castle*.

Below: bear effigy in the graveyard
Bottom: Dacre Church

DACRE

At ★★ **Dacre Church**, you can go bear hunting. In the corners of the graveyard are stone effigies known as the ★★ **bears,** which may have adorned the castle, or possibly marked the corner boundaries of a much older burial ground. The stones are much eroded and some believe that they represent lions, not bears. With this in mind look closely for the faint outline of what could be a mane on one of the effigies. In any case, you may follow the story of a 'bear' leaning on a 'ragged staff' (northwest of the churchyard), then the bear attacked by a creature (a lynx?) on its back, and next reaching back to grab the cat. The last bear is in the course of consuming its attacker. The Norman church stands on an Anglian site with clear views of Dacre Castle from the churchyard.

From Dacre, head for the A66 or the A592 to Penrith.

3: Tarn Hows and Potter Country

Ambleside – Coniston – Tarn Hows – Hawkshead – Sawrey – Windermere Ferry – Ambleside (20 miles/32km)

Star Attraction
● Dacre Church and bears

Those who think of Lancashire as being an area of dingy towns with forests of mill chimneys might reflect during this journey that for many centuries before local government was reorganised in 1974, most of the Lake District area belonged to the Red Rose County – yet it is a glorious area of gentle hills, lakes and tarns, woodland, white-walled farms and cottages. During a royal visit to the Lake District, the Queen had afternoon tea at one of the little whitewashed farms in Yewdale. Beatrix Potter met Peter Rabbit at Near Sawrey.

Tarn Hows, which is frequently portrayed in books and on picture postcards as an example of scenic Lakeland, has a haunting beauty despite being in a sense man-made. The water is retained by a dam to regulate its flow to the Monk Coniston estate. The trees, upstart conifers, impart a resinous smell.

Arthur Ransome
Our route takes in part of Arthur Ransome Country. The author belonged to a Leeds family, and the holidays of his boyhood were spent at Nibthwaite, near the outflow of Coniston Water. He was in the Yewdale area on a protracted holiday in 1908 when he came up with the story of *Swallows and Amazons*. One of the Yewdale farms is described in his novel *Winter Holiday*. His *Swallows and Amazons* was inspired by memories of boating on Windermere and Coniston Water. In two of his books, the *Gondola* became a houseboat. The great hill Wetherlam, which dominates the Yewdale valley, appears in *Swallowdale* and *Pigeon Post*.

LOUGHRIGG FELL

The A593 from **Ambleside** runs to the south of the sprawling, multi-turreted **Loughrigg Fell**, which is deserving of a visit by itself. Obtain a leaflet at the Bridge House, Ambleside, relating to a 2½-mile (4-km) nature saunter on the Fell, from which there are stunning views of Ambleside and Rydal Water.

The A593, in its meanderings, offers glimpses of the **River Brathay** (a Norse name for a broad river), which gathers up near the Three Shires Stone on Wrynose Pass and has transfusions of cold beck water from Little Langdale before presenting a white-water spectacle near **Skelwith Bridge**.

There is a National Trust car park south of Loughrigg Tarn. It is but a short walk to ★ **Skelwith Force** ('the noisy fall').

Loughrigg Tarn

Map on page 18

YEWDALE

The road to Coniston now climbs between tracts of indigenous woodland at the verge of the crags of the Borrowdale volcanics. A roadside tarn on the right, backed up by conifers, gives the journey a backwoods flavour. The road dips into **Yewdale** (valley of the yew trees), which is owned by the National Trust. Wordsworth described the valley as 'An area level as a Lake and spread/Under a rock too steep for man to tread. The 17th-century farms are architecturally outstanding…'

CONISTON

At **Coniston**, the presiding mountain is **The Old Man of Coniston** (2,635ft/803m), which can be climbed on a well-marked route from the village by good walkers who, in chancy weather, have waterproof clothing. On the way up are many traces of mining and quarries for slate.

The presiding spirit at Coniston is John Ruskin, whose grave at ★ **St Andrew's Church** has a Celtic-style cross of Tilberthwaite stone, with a design (reflecting his many interests) devised by his secretary and good friend, W.G. Collingwood, another notable writer. Collingwood shares the glory with Ruskin in the ★★ **Ruskin Museum**, founded in 1900 and renovated in 1999 (Easter–mid-Nov, 10am–5.30pm, Nov–Easter,

Gondola
The Victorian steam-yacht *Gondola* still cruises on Coniston Water to a regular timetable and with a full head of steam. It calls at a pier at Brantwood, home to John Ruskin, the great Victorian thinker, writers' artist and social reformer. Brantwood overlooks Coniston Water and the Coniston Fells, one of the finest views in England.

Cruising on Coniston

Wed–Sun 10.30am–3.30pm). The Museum is a few minutes' walk from the church. Ruskin lived at Brantwood, east of Coniston Water, from 1872 until his death in 1900.

★★ **Brantwood** (daily Mar–mid-Nov, 11am –5.30pm, mid-Nov–March 11am–4.30pm) may be reached by road from Coniston (B5285) or, as indicated, by the steam yacht ★★*Gondola*, which sails from Coniston Pier (signposted from the village; daily Easter–Oct, weather permitting, first sailing 11am). If the weather is chilly, visitors can find shelter in the upholstered saloon. The design for this 1859 steam launch was approved by that great arbiter of good taste, John Ruskin. It lay wrecked in Nibthwaite Bay for many years but was rescued by the National Trust and given an extensive restoration. Notice how the steam engine is responsive and quiet as the craft glides through the water.

TARN HOWS

A view of ★★★ **Tarn Hows**, northeast of Coniston, appears on virtually every calendar with a Lake District content, and is almost as familiar to a Lakeland enthusiast as the back of the hand. Even so, like the *Mona Lisa*, it might be visited time and again without mental weariness. Tarn Hows is reached by turning left from the Coniston–Hawkshead road (B5285) down a signposted byroad. A one-way system is in operation. There is adequate car parking provided by the National Trust, including a car park for disabled people that is much closer to the lake. A good footpath leads around the tarn, which was created about a century ago by building a dam and merging three tarns. The views from the southern side of the lake, where the path takes to higher ground, are quite magnificent.

COURTHOUSE

The exit road links with the Coniston-Hawkshead road. Turn left for Hawkshead. Near the junction with the Ambleside road is the ★ **Courthouse**

Star Attractions
● Ruskin Museum
● Tarn Hows
● Brantwood

Below: Ruskin's grave
Bottom: Tarn Hows

Map on page 18

(late Mar–Oct, daily 11am–4pm, access by key from the National Trust Shop, The Square, Hawkshead). This distinguished building is all that remains of a range of 15th-century manorial buildings associated with Furness Abbey. The Courthouse holds an exhibition relating to local life.

HAWKSHEAD

Traffic has virtually been eliminated from the narrow streets and squares of **Hawkshead**. A reflection of the popularity of this wonderful little town, with its white-painted buildings, its narrow streets, yards and alleys, is the difficulty in finding space in the large car park.

The ★★ **Old Grammar School** (founded 1585 by Archbishop Edwin Sandys but no longer used as such) is open to the public (April–Oct, Mon–Sat, noon–1pm 2–5pm, Sun 1–5.30pm). William Wordsworth received part of his education (1779–87) here, and he carved his initials on his desk. He lodged with Mistress Tyson either at Hawkshead or nearby Colthouse (there were Tysons in both places). He enjoyed walking and also raven-watching, recalling: *Oh! when I have hung/Above the raven's nest, by knots of grass/And half-inch fissures in the slippery rock…*

The poet Wordsworth now takes second place at Hawkshead to Beatrix Potter, whose spirit

St Michael's Church
The most prominent building in Hawkshead is St Michael's Church, a large and handsome structure indicative of 15th-century prosperity, the inner walls adorned with murals and painted texts dating from the 17th century. The Church is the venue for musical occasions on certain summer Sundays. When viewed from the knoll, the whitewashed houses of the old town appear to huddle. Each building seems to have its unique style, which is why a person is inclined to return again and again.

The Courthouse

broods over several shops specialising in her books and related souvenirs, and at the National Trust's ★ **Beatrix Potter Gallery** (early mid-Mar–Oct, Sat–Thurs 10.30am–4pm; admission by timed ticket). The gallery occupies offices used by Beatrix's solicitor husband, William Heelis. There is an annually changing exhibit of original sketches and watercolours painted by the multi-talented Beatrix.

Star Attractions
● **Old Grammar School**
● **Hill Top**

ESTHWAITE WATER

A short distance along the lakeside road is a right turn for Grizedale *(see page 77)*. **Esthwaite Water** (which means 'lake by the eastern clearing') is 1½ miles (2km) long. The young Wordsworth often began a new day by walking round the lake, being back in time for school; he also skated on Esthwaite Water. The lake has a pastoral setting and now sustains a trout fishery.

Below and Bottom: Beatrix Potter's Hill Top

SAWREY

Follow the B5285 from Hawkshead to **Near Sawrey**. Beatrix Potter's first Lake District holiday with her family was at Wray Castle, a Victorian spoof edifice near Windermere. She grew so fond of this quiet part of what was then North Lancashire that she used the royalties from her first book, *The Tale of Peter Rabbit*, published in 1900, to purchase ★★ **Hill Top** (early April–Nov, Sat–Wed, Good Friday, times vary according to season. Telephone booking possible 015394-36269). Being one of the major attractions of the Lake District, and relatively small, a limited number of visitors will be admitted at any one time. When she married William Heelis, they resided in **Castle Cottage** (private) in Near Sawrey.

Follow the road to **Far Sawrey**. The large car-carrying **Windermere Ferry** that now plies the lake is held on course by metal cables stretched from shore to shore. The journey takes only a few minutes. The ferry does not operate in the winter months.

Return to **Ambleside** by the A592 and the A591.

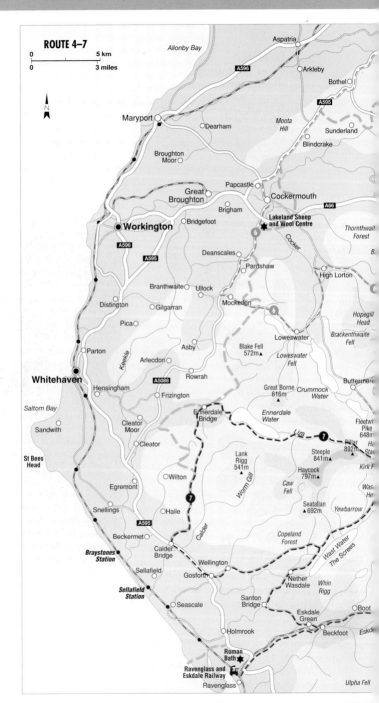

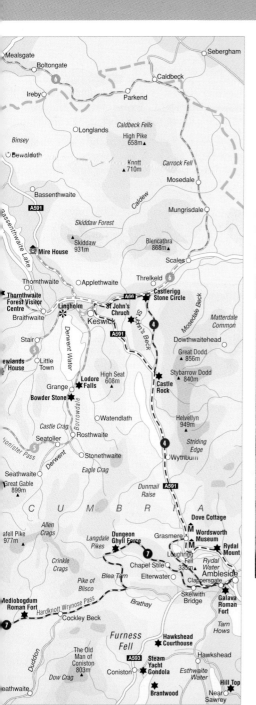

*Below: encounter
near Caldbeck
Bottom: Keswick Gardens*

Map
on pages
42–3

4: Keswick to St John's in the Vale

Keswick – Castlerigg – Thirlmere – Dunmail Raise – Grasmere – Rydal Water – Ambleside – St John's in the Vale – Keswick (31 miles/50km)

Keswick, northern capital of the Lakes, presides over Derwent Water and Bassenthwaite Lake, with Skiddaw (locally pronounced *Skidder*) clearing the 3,000-ft / 900-m contour. Climbing the fell is not difficult, just protracted, and people usually start from Millbeck, near Applethwaite, or from Latrigg. Charles Lamb enthused after climbing it in 1802: 'O its fine black head & the bleak air a top of it, with the prospect of mountains all about & about, making you giddy…' Blencathra, its neighbour, provides a backdrop for the sprawling village of Threlkeld.

Romantic allure
As the Romantic Age developed towards the end of the 18th century, Keswick became allied with tourism. Coleridge noted in 1800 that 'for two thirds of the year we are in complete retirement – the other third is alive & swarms with Tourists of all shapes & sizes & characters.'

KESWICK

Keswick retains a strong Victorian appearance which belies its age. The name is Old English for 'cheese farm', the K being a dash of Old Norse. View Derwent Water in its setting of fells and woodland and then try to imagine the conditions over 1,300 years ago, when Herbert, a Christian saint, became a hermit on one of the islands. About AD550, Kentigern, hearing that 'many among the mountains were given to idolatry',

Derwentwater

erected a cross as a sign of faith at Crosfeld (Crosthwaite). Leland (1540) arrived to find 'a lytle poore market town cawled Keswike'. Soon afterwards, the place was industrialised with the arrival of German miners. They were employed to seek gold, but in the end they mined copper. Graphite, discovered in the 16th century and mined in the Seathwaite valley at the head of Borrowdale, has always been useful, but with the arrival of the pencil, Keswick assumed world eminence as a centre of pencil production. Tourism was the next boom.

HALLS AND MUSEUMS

Keswick has a **Moot Hall** (market hall) which has the grand lines and spired tower of a church (with a one-handed clock) and rises from a traffic island in an area almost entirely devoted to tourism. The Moot Hall itself holds a tourist information centre. Keswick's ★★ **Museum and Art Gallery** (early Mar–Oct, Tues–Sat 10am–4pm) has a handy situation in Fitz Park and is a good starting point for anyone with an interest in local traditions. Purpose-built from green volcanic slate, the museum has a delightful Victorian flavour. Among the exhibits are a scale model of the Lake District (1834), letters by the poets Wordsworth and Southey, and Hugh Walpoles' manuscripts.

Greta Hall, the home of Samuel Taylor Coleridge in 1800–03 and of Robert Southey in 1803–43, is now a private home offering bed and breakfast (tel: 017687 75980). Of wide interest is the ★★ **Cumberland Pencil Museum** (daily 9.30am–4pm). Entertaining displays (including the world's largest colouring pencil) relate to the mining of graphite and the making of pencils.

CASTLERIGG

Leave Keswick on the A591 and call at ★★★ **Castlerigg**, which is well signposted. Here, set on a hill with a wondrous panorama of greater

Star Attractions
● **Museum and Art Gallery**
● **Cumberland Pencil Museum**
● **Castlerigg**

Below: shopping in Keswick
Bottom: Castlerigg stone circle

Map on pages 42–3

hills all around, 48 well preserved grey stones form an oval (not a true circle) about a 100ft (30m) across. Other stones form a rectangle to the east of the main group.

Was Castlerigg the centre of a tribal territory? No one knows. To the Victorian tourists, this was a haunt of Druids, but Castlerigg probably dates back to the much earlier Bronze Age. Wordsworth wrote in 1818 of '*a dismal cirque/Of Druid stones upon a forlorn moor.*'

Swirral Edge, Helvellyn

THIRLMERE AND HELVELLYN

The A591 unfolds under the gaze of high fells. **Castle Rock** *(see page 50)* guards the entrance to St John's in the Vale on the left. The Dodds, crowning the skyline, are to the north of mighty **Helvellyn** (3,116ft/950m; *see page 31*). Steepness does not deter modern walkers, and **Thirlspot Inn** on the left is one of several starting points from which an ascent of Helvellyn might begin.

Thirlmere, 4 miles (6km) long, may be circumnavigated by the motorist. A plaque on the dam commemorates the beginning of work on the reservoir (22 August 1890), which grew from two small lakes, Leathe's Water and Wythburn Water. The dam holds the water to a depth of 50ft (16m) – more than the level of the natural lakes. Thirlmere feeds the watertaps of Manchester, some 90 miles (56km) to the south. At times of low water, the bare shoreline may appear unsightly, but the plantations that once stood like battalions of soldiers at attention are more varied now. Red deer inhabit the woodlands west of the water, and they summer on the open fells beyond.

WYTHBURN CHURCH

★★ **Wythburn Church** (pronounced Wyburn, meaning a valley where willow trees grow) is visible on the eastern side of the A591. The building, long, low and predominantly 17th-century, has retained the old Lake District flavour. Near the church, visitors making the steep ascent of Helvellyn may park their cars.

ANCIENT PASS

Rejoin the A591 for a crossing of the watershed at **Dunmail Raise**. This ancient pass between Thirlmere and Grasmere has been improved for motorists by a stretch of dual carriageway. A cairn at the top, between the carriageways, explains the name of the pass. It marks where Dunmail, the last king of Cumberland, was defeated in AD945 by Edmund, King of Northumbria.

Dunmail Raise was, until 1974, on the border of Cumberland and Westmorland. There is a good view of the rugged 'mane' of **Helm Crag** (right) from the lay-by on Dunmail Raise. Reaching the summit demands rock-climbing skill and nerve. Wainwright, in his pictorial guide to the area, left a space on which he might write the date of his ascent, but he never managed that last awkward bit.

Coachmen driving four-in-hands from Windermere to Keswick entertained tourists by giving names to unusual rocks, the most notable being the **Lion and the Lamb**, at the southern end of the ridge.

The Raise allows people to hear as well as see further. In the early 19th century, during the Peninsular War, Thomas De Quincey (one of the Wordsworth coterie) and William Wordsworth walked up the Raise from Grasmere, at about midnight, to meet the Keswick carrier and the London papers. They had advance notice of his approach when Wordsworth lay on the ground

Star Attraction
● **Wythburn Church**

> **Woodland trails**
> Nature trails are to be found in the woodland on either side of Thirlmere. A car park that is also a good observation point is situated on the right-hand side of the A591.

Dunmail Raise

Map
on pages
42–3

and listened. De Quincey said this was so he might 'catch any sound of wheels that might be groaning along at a distance.'

GRASMERE

Grasmere, the heart of 'Wordsworthshire', has two large car parks, one of which is adjacent to Stock Lane and quite close to the field in which the **Grasmere Sports** have been held in August for over 130 years. There were traffic problems when Beatrix Potter visited the Sports in 1895, for she was a late arrival 'and had difficulty in finding friends among the crowd of carriages'. Lord Lonsdale, arriving via Kirkstone Pass in a yellow-painted coach, took special interest in the Cumberland and Westmorland style of wrestling, on which he was an authority.

Below: Grasmere village
Bottom: Dove Cottage

Wordsworth effusively wrote that Grasmere was 'the loveliest spot that man hath ever found'. Grasmere (the lake, that is, complete with island and rowing boats) lies in what he called 'a mountain urn'. The Vale of Grasmere is virtually ringed by shapely fells, of which the most prominent is Helm Crag. The novelist E.M. Forster, who stayed in the village in the summer of 1907, liked the place though he said 'it rains all night and every day, but not always all day.'

There is plenty for non-literary day trippers to do, for Grasmere is half full of little shops. The more studious visitors make for ★★ **St Oswald's**

Church, which still is (as it was in Wordsworth's time, 1799–1813) a structure *of rude and antique majesty [with] pillars crowded and the roof upheld / By naked rafters intricately crossed / like leafless underboughs in some thick wood.* The annual Rushbearing on the Saturday nearest 5 August *(see page 83)* was a feature of the poet's day, for he saw children, each with a garland, walking through the still churchyard, noting that the garland was carried 'like a sceptre and o'ertops the head of the proud bearer.' Pilgrims form respectful knots before the Wordsworthian graves.

Star Attractions
● St Oswald's Church
● Dove Cottage
● Wordsworth Museum

DOVE COTTAGE

★★★**Dove Cottage** (daily 9.30am–5pm, closed 24–26 December and early Jan–early Feb), home of William Wordsworth and his sister Dorothy during his early, highly creative years, stands just to the east of the A591, in an area known as Town End.

The white-washed cottage is now hemmed in by much later buildings. The Wordsworths had a view directly over Grasmere and on to the fells, as Dorothy noted in December, 1801: 'We played at cards – sat up late. The moon shone upon the water below Silver-How... Wm lay with his curtains open that he might see it.' The cottage was the Wordsworths' home from 1799–1808. It was a time dedicated to plain living and high thinking. Dove Cottage is particularly appealing in cold weather, when a bright fire burns in the grate.

In the adjacent ★★**Wordsworth Museum**, a barn conversion, a permanent exhibition recounting the Wordsworth story is backed up by special exhibitions. Dove Cottage has a reciprocal discount scheme operated with Rydal Mount and Wordsworth House at Cockermouth.

Grasmere and Rydal Water are connected by a footpath along **Loughrigg Terrace**. The path can be reached directly from Dove Cottage along a causeway by the road that offers unhindered views of the lake and Helm Crag or via a wood called Bainbriggs, a favourite pre-tea walk of the Wordsworths. Alternatively, use the large car park near the church, and walk around the other side of

Parking
Dove Cottage has its own small car park, but as the space is always in keen demand it is recommended that the large car park in Stock Lane (B5287) is used, from where it is just a few minutes' walk to the cottage.

Wordsworth relics at Dove Cottage

Map
on pages
42–3

Nab Cottage

Across Rydal Water, once secluded, but now a guest house and training centre in a lay-by of the A591, is Nab Cottage. Thomas De Quincey lodged here and then married Peggy Simpson, daughter of his landlord. Wordsworth thought that Thomas could have done better, but the happy couple remained happy. The De Quinceys moved to Wordsworth's old cottage at Grasmere, and into Nab Cottage came Hartley Coleridge, the son of Samuel Taylor Coleridge.

Rydal Mount

the lake. After a little road work, a footpath is found which leads to the south of the two lakes.

Rydal Water, which is smaller than Grasmere, is a reedy lake, with several islands and a population of waterfowl. Red squirrels might be seen in the larches. The view for much of the year is given a ginger hue by the dead bracken fronds. ★★ **Rydal Mount** (daily in summer 9.30am–5pm, winter Wed–Mon 10am–4pm) is at the head of the village, near the start of a footpath leading back to Grasmere. William Wordsworth lived here from 1813 until his death in 1850. A descendant now owns the house. After a brief introductory talk, visitors may wander around the house and 4½-acre (2-hectare) garden, which was landscaped by Wordsworth. During summer, refreshments are served in a marquee and picnics lunches can be arranged (tel: 015394 33002).

★ **Rydal Church**, a 19th-century structure with a memorial to Dr Thomas Arnold, his wife and son Matthew, is adjacent to ★ **Dora's Field**, which Wordsworth bought and gave to his daughter, Dora. Unhappily, she died and the field reverted to Wordsworth. Pilgrims in April walk between expanses of daffodils and narcissi – if the sheep haven't got to them first. **Rydal Hall**, home of the Le Flemings in Wordsworth's day, is now a conference and study centre for Carlisle Diocese. The garden and tea shop are open to the public, and a footpath to Ambleside passes through the park.

ST JOHN'S IN THE VALE

Motor into **Ambleside** *(see page 34)*, follow the town's one-way system and take the A593 through Clappersgate. Turn right before Skelwith Bridge and the junction with the B5343, up a signposted road that crosses **Red Bank** (which has a fine view of Grasmere lake) and back to Grasmere town. Take the A591 back over Dunmail Raise to Thirlmere.

The B5322 leaves the A591 for **St John's in the Vale**. The crag on the right is known as **Castle Rock**, and it greatly impressed early tourists. William Hutchinson (1774) compared it with 'an ancient ruined castle' which, as they drew near, 'changed its figure, and proved no other than a shaken massive pile of rocks.' Walter Scott, shown the rock and having read Hutchinson's account, wrote *The Bridal of Triermaine*, a poem in which King Arthur finds the castle deserted, rouses it with a bugle blast and brings it back to life, complete with 'a band of damsels fair'.

To motor down this vale when the high fells are powdered with snow is to enjoy an alpine spectacle, for the eye goes directly to **Blencathra** (2,847ft/868m), which appears to block out half the sky. John Ruskin, who climbed Blencathra in 1867, thought of it as 'the finest thing I've yet seen, there being several bits of real crag-work and a fine view at the top over the great plain of Penrith on one side, and the Cumberland hills, as a chain, on the other. Fine fresh wind blowing, and plenty of crows.'

Star Attractions
● Rydal Mount
● St John's in the Vale Church

St John's in the Vale Church
Two miles down this valley, look for the sign to ★★ **St John's in the Vale Church**. A narrow road leads to the church, which sits snugly behind yew trees in the shadow of a steep hill. A church on the site was mentioned in a document dated 1554, but the present structure dates from 1845. One of the finely lettered tombstones in the churchyard relates to John Richardson (1817–86), whose poems in the Lakeland dialect are still much enjoyed.

At **Threlkeld** go left to **Keswick** via the A66.

Below: Rydal Water
Bottom: Wordsworth's library

Map on pages 42–3

5: The Borrowdale Round

Keswick – Grange – Rosthwaite – Honister Pass – Great Gable – Buttermere – Newlands (20 miles/32km)

Canon Rawnsley, a Victorian parson of Keswick, considered there was 'no better five shillings' worth of carriage driving at the Lakes than can be enjoyed by all who gather in the Keswick Market Place on a fine morning at ten o'clock and take their seats on any of the char-a-bancs waiting to convey them up Borrowdale, thence home by the Newlands Vale.' Able-bodied passengers were asked to walk up steep hills. On descents, a squeal emanated from a 'slipper' or wedge of wood on which a wheel rode. It was a primitive but effective braking device. Coach-drivers gave a commentary on what was to be seen and related stories of local daftness. The Borrovians (if such is the term) were said to have constructed a wall across the bottom of the valley to restrain the cuckoo and ensure everlasting summer.

Borrowdale, to many the most scenic of the Lakeland valleys, offers some demanding crags for rock-climbing and walkers move jauntily along its airy ridges.

Looking-glass lake
Derwent Water mirrors a range of handsome fells and also the Jaws of Borrowdale, best seen from Friars Crag (on the right as you leave Keswick; it is an easy walk from the car park). As well as pleasure craft, there is a regular boat service to various jetties, and lakeside walks are well laid out. Of the islands, St Herbert's had the hermitage of a Celtic saint. Derwent Island became the home of German immigrants in the 16th century, whose skills as miners were needed to recover local copper.

Lodore Falls

LODORE FALLS

The B5289 is the name given to the romantic road that runs through Borrowdale to Buttermere. The road leaves Keswick to skirt **Derwent Water**, the 'queen' of English lakes, which has a maximum depth of 72ft (22m), but looks shallow.

Near the head of Derwent Water, behind the Lodore Falls Hotel and accessible on payment of a small charge, are the ★★**Lodore Falls**, about which Robert Southey wrote *The Cataract of Lodore* (1820), first asking *how does the water come down…?*, then answering in a style which is now familiar to most Lakeland visitors, including: *Collecting, projecting/Receding and speeding/And shocking and rocking/And darting and parting…* A visit to the falls is exciting in wet spells. It is said that an American, after looking for them for several hours, sat down and asked a passer-by, 'Say, where are the Lodore Falls?' They informed him that he was sitting on them!

Star Attraction
● Lodore Falls

GRANGE-IN-BORROWDALE

Grange-in-Borrowdale (*grange* because this is where the granary of Furness Abbey was located) is reached over a narrow, double bridge. The ★ **church** is picturesque both inside and out. About a mile from Grange on the road running west of Derwent Water stands **Brackenburn**, a private house that was owned by Hugh Walpole, author of *The Herries Chronicle,* three books published in the 1930s, about a Cumberland boy. Though private, its main features can be seen from the road, and above the garage, where he had a study decked by 30,000 books, is a blue plaque commemorating Walpole's association. To him, this was a 'little paradise on Cat Bells', the hill looming beyond. Water drawn from deep in the fell has the tingle effect of good wine.

Grange is a good point from which to walk beside the river and through the famous Borrowdale oak woodland. The species of oak is the north country 'sessile', a reference to the stalkless acorns. The **River Derwent** has a green appearance – the water is pure and the bed of the river is composed primarily of pieces of greenish slate.

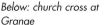

Below: church cross at Grange
Bottom: Borrowdale valley

Map on pages 42–3

BOULDERS AND SCREE

Continue on the B5289 to where there is parking near a sign heralding the ★★ **Bowder Stone**, an enormous boulder with a length of 62ft (19m) and a height of 36ft (11m). A wooden ladder with rails, fixed against the side of the stone, gives access to its summit.

The road continues, pent-in between **King's How** (named after Edward VII) and ★ **Castle Crag**, which looms above the oak woods on the west bank and is best approached from Grange. Climbing its steep scree slope is not to be undertaken lightly, but with care visitors can reach a supreme vantage point with magnificent views overlooking the oak-wooded valley, Derwent Water and Skiddaw.

Rosthwaite, a village with a car park and toilets, has a post office with a village store that is popular with visitors. The village is at the start of a footpath leading over the fell to the remote hamlet of **Watendlath**.

Of special interest, west of the river and between Rosthwaite and Seatoller, is the lovely oak woodland, **Johnny Wood**, in which there is a nature trail.

Seatoller
From Rosthwaite there is ready access to the riverside with a walk up the dale to Seatoller, a cluster of attractive buildings, some erected for quarrymen when the Honister mines were first opened. The National Park authority converted a barn into a base with a garden, picnic area, displays and study facilities. Craft workers visit the base to give demonstrations.

Bowder Stone

EAGLE CRAG

Stonethwaite to the left is a hamlet worth exploring, and walking up the dale for a short distance brings **Eagle Crag** into view. Rosthwaite and Stonethwaite were named by Norse settlers for the amount of stone lying about, all of which had to be cleared before cultivation.

The eagles of Eagle Crag were persecuted, as were ravens. Churchwardens' accounts reveal that a bounty was paid on dead birds. The traveller Gray, visiting Grange-in-Borrowdale in 1769, heard from a farmer how the previous year he plundered the eyrie of the golden eagles: 'He was let down in ropes to the shelf of the rock on which the nest was built, the people above shouting and holloaing to fright the old birds, which flew screaming round, but did not dare to attack him'

GRAPHITE MINES

The dale peters out at **Seathwaite Farm**, a mile south of Seatoller, left down a side road. The wettest inhabited farm in England (125 inches/3,175mm a year), four generations of Edmondsons have farmed Seathwaite. There is roadside parking, a sheep farm, trout farm and a small café. A short walk from Seathwaite Farm is **Stockley Bridge**, a packhorse-type bridge on the route from Borrowdale to Wasdale. There is also a track from Seathwaite barn across the valley to a river bridge, from which an approach may be made to waterfalls in **Sour Milk Ghyll**. On the hillside are remains of the old graphite mines (which must not be explored because of potential danger). When a pure form of graphite was discovered here in the 16th century, it had various uses. Being rare and of practical value, including making metal castings and cannon balls, it was treated like gold. In the early 19th century, guards were posted at the mines and workmen were searched before they left. Graphite was eventually to be used extensively in Keswick's pencil industry.

SLATE QUARRIES

Able-bodied men taking the Borrowdale Coach Round in the 19th century had to walk up **Honister Pass** (1,190ft/362m) from Seatoller. Canon Rawnsley, arriving at the head of the pass, saw

Star Attraction
● Bowder Stone

Below: the Honister Pass
Bottom: the road to Seatoller

Map on pages 42–3

Honister Crag, which 'gleams at us as if some great earth painter had been grinding up grey slate and mixed it with emerald and begun to wash in his colour from skyline to the valley bottom.' The slate quarried up here was composed of the compacted dust and ash from volcanic activity. A rough track now runs up the side of Honister Crag, and there is little to indicate that the whole fell is honeycombed by shafts and galleries. For a time, it was customary to pack slate on long sledges and run with the sledges down the screes to the roadside below. The sledgeman then had to climb back with his sledge for another load.

Fell walkers park their cars beside Honister Pass when following a comparatively easy route to the summit of **Great Gable** (2,949ft/899m). On Remembrance Sunday, many gather on Great Gable to remember those who fell in two world wars. They stand beside a memorial to those members of the Fell and Rock Climbing Club who were victims in the conflicts.

BUTTERMERE BEAUTY

The road descends from the heights of Honister to **Buttermere** lake, which is reached at Gatesgarth Farm at the foot of shapely **Fleetwith Pike** (2,126ft/648m). A car park just across the road from the farm is handy for those who wish to explore the dalehead. Others go on to the **Fish**

Alfred Wainwright

On a window ledge in Buttermere Church is a plaque in memory of Alfred Wainwright, the most famous of fellwalkers and author of the idiosyncratic Pictorial Guides to the Lake District fells. Look through the window on a clear day and the fell named Haystacks is in view. On his death in 1991, Wainwright's ashes were scattered on Haystacks at his particular request.

Boating on Buttermere

Hotel at Buttermere village, where (wrote Joseph Budworth in 1792), 'If you are fond of strong ale, I must tell, Buttermere is reckoned famous for it.' The tale is told of Mary Robinson, the 'Buttermere Beauty'; she was the daughter of a landlord of the Fish Hotel in the early 19th century and was noted for her looks. Budworth saw her: 'She brought in part of our dinner, and seemed to be about fifteen. Her hair was thick and long, of a dark brown, and, though unadorned with ringlets, did not seem to want them; her face was a fine oval, with full eyes and lips as red as vermillion; her cheeks had more of the lily than of the rose.' Mary attracted the attention of a 'gentleman' who introduced himself as the Hon. Alexander Hope MP, brother of the Earl of Hopetoun. They were married in 1802. Unfortunately, the Hon. Alexander turned out to be John Hatfield, an imposter, bigamist, forger and bankrupt. His iniquities led to him being hanged at Carlisle. The Buttermere Beauty later married a local farmer.

Below and Bottom: Buttermere Church and blossoms in the yard

NEWLANDS

It is possible to walk around Buttermere lake, though one of its features, a tunnel cut in living rock, has been closed for safety reasons. When Rawnsley did the 'Buttermere Round', a break was arranged for lunch at Buttermere village. There was time to visit 'the tiny church, with its 12 steps in memory of the Apostles'. Follow the road up past the church for the third and final leg of the journey. **Newlands Hause** used to warm up the coach horses, and the most athletic passengers would be asked to walk beside the coach in order to lighten the load. **Newlands** is a secluded valley, almost a basin among fells, with many farms and two tiny hamlets, Stair and Littletown, the last-named being well-known to Beatrix Potter, who included drawings of it in *The Tale of Mrs Tiggy-winkle*. The mine levels driven into the flanks of **Catbells** and **Maiden Moor** were worked in the days of Queen Elizabeth I. They yielded copper, lead and even a little gold.

Map on pages 42–3

6: Around Skiddaw

Keswick – Mungrisdale – Caldbeck – Cockermouth – Crummock Water – Whinlatter (60 miles/97km)

Old Skiddaw tops the 3,000-ft (900-m) contour and sprawls over an area of 14 sq miles (36 sq km). Walkers who cross the fell or follow a good path from near the old Sanatorium at Threlkeld to Skiddaw House sample an austere landscape 'Back o' Skidder'. Almost every creature that breathes is a sheep. Skiddaw House, built for the use of shepherds, is now a youth hostel in season, with an out-room available to anyone in need of shelter.

Skiddaw slate gives this northern fell country some grand sweeping lines, as anyone can see who follows a cul-de-sac from Mosedale beside the River Caldew to what remains of mining days at the highly mineralised hill called Carrock Fell. Those who walk the hills can look far south into the valley containing Thirlmere.

In the churchyard of Caldbeck lie the mortal remains of huntsman John Peel, who inspired a world-famous song. (Incidentally, he had a coat so *grey* – the undyed wool of the Herdwick sheep). Westwards lies the market town of Cockermouth and classic Lake District terrain, with soaring fells admiring their reflections in Loweswater and Crummock Water.

Below: Old Skiddaw in the distance
Bottom: on Carrock Fell

PERILOUS HEIGHT

The A66 east of Keswick is dominated by **Blencathra** (2,847ft/868m, *see page 51*), a fell empurpled by flowering heather in late summer. Walkers who use the Threlkeld car park and start with a walk through the fields at the foot of the great hill usually pick the path on the arête that leads directly to the summit. In a strong wind, avoid this route. Coleridge, one of the Lakeland Poets, appreciated the power of moving air: *On stern Blencathra's perilous height/The winds are tyrannous and strong;/And flashing forth unsteady light/From stern Blencathra's skiey height,/As loud the torrents throng!*

Leave the A66 for **Mungrisdale**, where the ★ **church**, dedicated to St Kentigern, is an architectural treasure dating from the 18th century, long, low, whitewashed and containing a three-decker pulpit dated 1679. The clerk sat on the lower deck while the parson took the service from the second deck and preached from the top deck. Drive on through Mosedale into an area which gives the feel of the big country Back o' Skiddaw. The valley itself is scenic, with the atmosphere of a Scottish glen – boulders, heather and a brawling beck, crossed at one point by a private bridge that gives access to a walk to **Bowscale Tarn**, in a grand setting of fells.

Where the road peters out, there is the remains of a mine at **Carrock Fell** (2,174ft/662m). In 1857, Carrock was visited by Charles Dickens and Wilkie Collins, though local people had told them no visitors ever went up that hill. The two men had arrived on a wet day, and at the top, in mist and rain, they had a magnificent view of nothing.

CALDBECK

On to **Caldbeck** (meaning cold stream). This area is a vast sheep range also frequented by some of the stocky, dark fell-type ponies once ridden by the shepherds and used for light farm work. Caldbeck, built largely of limestone, is on the northern boundary of the Lake District National Park. Ask locally for directions to the ★ **Howk**, a limestone gorge

Famous huntsman

John Peel – the huntsman, d'ye ken – was born at Park End in 1776 and interred in the Caldbeck churchyard in 1854. Hunting symbols are found on his gravestone, which is big, of a light tone and not far from the Church door. The words which have gone round the world in the song D'ye Ken John Peel were composed by John Woodcock Graves, a great friend of Peel who emigrated to Tasmania. Peel's portrait is kept in the Oddfellows' Arms. John Peel was first sung 'in the snug parlour' of Graves's house in the year 1824, to the tune of a Border rant called Bonnie Annie. An improved version of the music was devised in 1869 by William Metcalfe, the choir-master of Carlisle Cathedral. Metcalfe's tune survived.

Mungrisdale church

Map on pages 42–3

popularly thought of as a place for fairy revels, hence the alternative name Fairykirk. Caldbeck drew much of its former prosperity from industries powered by the fast-flowing River Caldew. Local people used to brag about their wealth: Caldbeck and Caldbeck Fells / Are worth all England else.

COCKERMOUTH

Take the B5299 over the back of the fell country to the A595 and turn left for **Cockermouth**, a market town that stands back from Lakeland proper, its red sandstone buildings emphasising its peripheral status. The town sits at the confluence of the rivers Cocker and Derwent and was given a market charter in 1221.

> **Cockermouth Castle**
> This stronghold was built in the 12th century to repulse Scottish raiders. During the Civil War, it held out for Parliament in 1648. The castle has suffered more from decay than from warlike forces. One of the wings, rebuilt in the 19th century, is still occupied. The castle is only open to the public on special occasions.

The broad, tree-lined main street is relatively quiet, having been by-passed by the A66. At the western end is the recently refurbished ★★ **Wordsworth House** (April–Oct, Mon–Fri 11am–4.30pm, Sat in high summer), now owned by the National Trust, where the poet was born in 1770. Wordsworth's father was steward to the Lonsdales. The house is furnished in the original style and some of the poet's personal effects are on display. Hands-on displays and characters in costume have been introduced. A memorial window to Wordsworth is to be found in **All Saints Church**, a Victorian structure with a 180-ft (55-m) spire and eight bells in the belfry. Close to the the castle is **Jennings Brewery**. Established over 150 years ago, the company moved to Cockermouth in 1874. The guided tour (Jan, Feb, Nov and Dec, daily 2pm, Mar, April, May, June, Mon–Sat 11am and 2pm) includes a sample of their real ales.

Horse-drawn Jennings Brewery dray, Cockermouth

MEET THE SHEEP

★ **The Lakeland Sheep and Wool Centre**, by the A66-A5086 roundabout, is open all year round (shows Mar–early Nov, Sun–Thurs 10.30am, noon, 2pm and 3.30pm). The centre is a hands-on opportunity for visitors to meet some of Cumbria's most famous residents. Nineteen different breeds of sheep are on view during the indoor presentations, and sheepdogs are put through their paces in a 300-seat arena. In season, shearing is part of the show. The centre has a café restaurant.

Star Attraction
● **Wordsworth House**

COASTAL TOWNS

Several villages in the Cockermouth area have produced famous men. Fletcher Christian, who mutinied on the *Bounty*, was born at Moorland Close in 1764. John Dalton of atomic theory fame was born in Eaglesfield in 1766. On the coast, **Maryport** harbour has been restored and has an attendant museum. Opposite the museum is *Fishy Tale* an amusing iron-ore sculpture.

Below: sheep shearing time
Bottom: Maryport Harbour

Whitehaven is a stimulating town, a redstone promontory with seabirds, handy to St Bees Head. The port's role in the rum trade unfolds at **The Rum Story** (daily 10am–4.30pm), set in the Jefferson family's 18th-century premises. Delve further into the area's history at **The Beacon** (daily 10am–4.30pm) with its five floors of interactive exhibits and galleries. A footpath leads from behind The Beacon to the **Haig Colliery Mining Museum** (daily 9.30am–4.30pm; tel: 01946 599949) on the former site of the Haig Pit. The pit's mighty steam winding engine is operated on most days and guided walks may be arranged.

At the **Helena Thompson Museum** in Workington are displays charting the maritime and social history of the town (Tues–Sun 1.30–4.30pm,

Map on pages 42–3

Jul–Aug 10.30am–4.30pm). **Workington Hall** in Curwen Park – refuge for Mary Queen of Scots during her last night of freedom in May 1568 – is a ruin, but plaques give visitors a flavour of the hall's long history, dating from the 14th century, when it was simply a pele tower.

Paint for a pint

Looming above the Swan Hotel, in a wooded area on the old road through Braithwaite and Thornthwaite (just before the A66), is the hill known as Barf (the pronumciation of Barugh, a north-country surname). The hotel rewards with a pint of ale a volunteer who regularly whitewashes the Bishop of Barf, a large stone marking the place where a man who fancied himself as a skilled horseman came to grief when attempting to ride up that side of the mountain. The area below the Bishop is mainly scree and unsound. A path approaches the summit from the side and back.

THORNTHWAITE FOREST

Leave Cockermouth on the A5086 and take a left turn for **Loweswater** ('leafy lake'). The road follows the shore of the mile-long lake and then on another half mile to the village of Loweswater, which is almost shadowed by **Mellbreak** (1,676ft/511m). **St Kentigern's Church** is not as old as the name suggests, having been rebuilt in Victorian times. Take the B5289 through Lorton Vale and drive to Buttermere village and back to enjoy fine views of **Crummock Water**.

Continue along the B5289 to High Lorton, and turn right at the B5292 for **Whinlatter Pass**, passing through Thornthwaite Forest with its ★★ **Visitor Centre** (summer 10am–5pm, winter 10am–4pm) with audio-visual presentation, details of various trails and cycle routes, and tea shop.

A vantage point by the road offers a good-weather view of **Bassenthwaite Lake** and Skiddaw. The lake is 4 miles (2.5km) long, a half mile (0.8km) wide and 51ft (16m) deep. There is a noisy side (the west) and a relatively quiet side. The noise is from traffic on the A66 to and from the industrialised towns of the west Cumbrian coast.

Loweswater fells

MIREHOUSE

Drive around the top of Bassenthwaite Lake via the B5291 and head back to Keswick on the A591. About 3½ miles (5km) before Keswick is - ★★ **Mirehouse** (April–Oct, grounds daily 10am–5.30pm, house Sun–Wed 2–4.30pm and Fri in Aug). This large family home, built in 1666, was last up for sale in 1688. It was extended in 1790, the additions including a stylish porch of red sandstone. Mirehouse has many connections with celebrities in the world of literature and art.

John Spedding lived here; he was a school friend of Wordsworth at Hawkshead. The poet Tennyson stayed at Mirehouse in 1835 and was reported to 'admire the country near the lakes very much, but could dispense with the deluges of sapping rains.' Some visitors stroll to the edge of Bassenthwaite Lake and look around **St Bega's**, an ancient church that was restored in Victorian times.

Star Attraction
● **Thornthwaite Forest Visitor Centre**
● **Mirehouse**

CROSTHWAITE CHURCH

Before driving into Keswick, visit ★ **Crosthwaite Church**, on the northern edge of the town, where the gateway is adorned by Celtic motifs designed by Canon Rawnsley (1851–1920), former vicar of Crosthwaite. Crosthwaite took its name from the cross erected in a clearing by St Kentigern *(see page 44)*. The first church would have been of wood and thatch, but traces of the Norman building that succeeded it are to be found in the north-aisle wall of the present church.

The 6th century was a good time for Keswick, judging by the extensions made to the church. In 1844 it was completely restored under the direction of Sir George Gilbert Scott. Look for the marble figure of Robert Southey (1774–1843), poet laureate at the time of Wordsworth who, incidentally, wrote an epitaph – and succeeded his friend as poet laureate. Southey's grave is on the north side of the church.

Bassenthwaite Lake

Map
on pages
42–3

7: The Western Lakes

Ambleside – Langdale Pikes – The High Passes – Wasdale Head – Ennerdale (60 miles/97km)

Great Langdale doesn't have a lake, but it has all the other attributes of a picturesque Lakeland valley – a beck, green fields hatched by dry-stone walls, and mountains blocking out more than half the sky. The passes of Wrynose and Hardknott are not for the timid, but they allow a motorist to go mountaineering without special effort.

The western Lake District is out of the way but worth the effort. One of the truly great sights is the Screes beyond Wastwater, preferably lit by a setting sun, draped like giant fans from a 1,700-ft (520-m) long cliff – the south-eastern buttress of sprawling Scafell. Elsewhere, the prominent features are sternness and sterility. As Thomas Wilkinson, a visitor in 1824, wrote: 'The mountains of Wast Water are naked to their base – their sides and their summits are uniform; their summits shoot up into lofty points and end in the form of pyramids.'

The Three Shires

At the summit of Wrynose is a stone pillar marked Lancashire' but known as Three Shires Stone. Here, before local government reorganisation in 1974, the counties of Cumberland, Westmorland and Lancashire were on nodding terms.

Great Langdale

GALAVA

Start from **Ambleside** *(see page 34)*. At Borrans, near the head of Windermere, stood a Roman fort named **Galava**. It was commented on by Cam-

den, who bravely entered these parts in 1586. He saw 'the carcase as it were of an ancient city with great ruins of walls, and of buildings without the walls still remaining scattered about.' Now there is just an expanse of grass. To visit the area is an appropriate prelude to the first part of this route, which takes in the high passes of Wrynose and Hardknott, where a Roman road connected them with Ravenglass, a natural harbour on the Cumbrian coast.

Below: Elterwater
Bottom: Elterwater's village shop

LANGDALE VALLEY

Follow the A593 through Skelwith Bridge *(see page 37)* and take the B5343 for Great Langdale, which bursts into view near **Elterwater**. Across the common and beyond the woodland rise the **Langdale Pikes**, one of the most distinctive landforms in the district. Elterwater has a large car park near the river bridge and a smaller car park (property of the National Trust) on the west side of the common, which is a grazing area for Herdwick sheep. The evidence of slate-quarrying is everywhere, and a terrace of slate dwellings overlooking the common is unusual and attractive. There are few visible remains of the old gunpowder factory that supplied the quarries. In its place is a large and attractive timeshare complex.

GREAT LANGDALE

Great Langdale proper is entered at **Chapel Stile**, in which the most prominent building is **Holy Trinity Church**. The church stands on a hill as though on a ledge, which means that church-going requires physical as well as spiritual stamina. In the churchyard is the grave of G.M. Trevelyan, author of *English Social History*, a classic book published in 1944.

Beyond the village, Thrang Crag and the residues of slate quarrying are prominent. So is a terrace of houses and holiday flats. A road to the quarry begins near a craft shop, but it is unwise to explore redundant quarries without taking local advice and wearing a stout helmet.

Map on pages 42–3

The Langdale Pikes dominate the dale with the impact of a Sphinx. Three fells are seen, these being **Harrison Stickle** (the highest, at 2,414ft/736m), **Pike o' Stickle** and **Pavey Ark**, and there are five summits in the group. The Pikes can be ascended, with some effort, from the New Dungeon Gill Hotel. Car parking seems ample, but in summer it is in the keenest demand. Near the foot of Pavey Ark's 600-ft (200-m) cliff is Stickle Tarn which, dammed in 1824, provided a constant head of water, via the river, for the gunpowder works at Elterwater.

Below: motorcycling over Wrynose Pass
Bottom: Ravenglass and Eskdale Railway

PASS OF THE STALLION

The road leaves the valley near **Wall End Farm**. Notice how large are some of the boulders in and beside the beck. The road climbs to **Blea Tarn**, in a secluded little valley, where an attractive farmhouse was the home of Solitary, a character in one of Wordsworth's poems. A car park to the left of the road is useful for anyone who wishes to use the footpath across the little valley. The car park is handy, too, for Blea Tarn, where there are trees and (a surprise) a grove of rhododendrons.

On reaching **Little Langdale**, turn right for the **Wrynose Pass**, sometimes referred to as 'pass of the stallion', the implication being that a strong horse was needed to negotiate it. Wrynose has a steep gradient, taking little time to attain 1,289ft (393m), and a reasonably good surface (because of work done after World War II, when it was used for military training).

ROMAN FORT AND STEAM RAILWAY

The road descends to the head of the **Duddon Valley**, where **Hardknott Pass** (more fearsome than Wrynose) begins its course to Eskdale with a steep gradient and a quick succession of hairpin bends, delivering the motorist to an elevation of 1,291ft (394m). Care is needed during the descent. Beside the road, on a plateau looking into Eskdale, are the considerable remains of ★★ **Mediobogdum**, a Roman fort. There is space beside the road on which to park the car. Wordsworth, in one of his sonnets about the River Duddon, pictured an eagle flying over the ruins of a fort 'whose guardians bent the knee to Jove and Mars'. **Eskdale**, though lakeless, extends with a quiet charm down to **Boot**, where the holiday spirits of many are buoyed up by the the **Ravenglass <u>and</u> Eskdale Railway** (affectionately known as 'Ratty').

At **Eskdale Green**, a narrow, unclassified road leads to **Santon Bridge** and on to **Nether Wasdale**, where the grandeur of **Wasdale** is unfolded. Alternatively, travel down to **Ravenglass**, where the Romans took advantage of a fine natural harbour. Here, Ratty, England's oldest narrow-gauge steam railway offers the chance to visit, in novel fashion, **Muncaster Water Mill**. The railway operates daily from March to October, with special days around Christmas and winter weekends.

WASDALE

On the journey through Wasdale, firstly there is a view of **Wastwater**, which has a cold, blue appearance. Wastwater is almost sterile and the least changed of the great lakes since they were formed by the scouring of glacial ice. The lake is very deep and in places extends below sea level. The famous **Screes**, to which reference has been made, are part of a 3-mile (5-km) cliff on a fell known as Illgill Head (1,998ft/608m). The road,

Star Attraction
● Mediobogdum

Shapely fells
Wasdale, its Screes and the dalehead with the pyramid of Great Gable all lie at the centre of a trinity of shapely fells. They make most sensitive people babble – but not Wordsworth, who described Wastwater matter-of-factly as long, narrow, stern and desolate'. Coleridge, in 1802, infused plenty of life and colour into his description of the Screes as 'consisting of fine red Streaks running in broad Stripes thro' a stone colour – slanting off from the Perpendicular, as steep as the meal newly ground from the Miller's Spout... like a pointed Decanter in shape, or an outspread fan.'

Wastwater

Map on pages 42–3

Below: Wasdale Head Show and Shepherds' Annual Meet
Bottom: Sphinx Rock, Great Gable

in places unfenced, stays close to the northern shore of the lake and is fringed by sheep-cropped herbage and gorse, the yellow blossoms of which enliven the district in spring. Where visitors stop, there are usually black-headed gulls, their raucous cries instilling a little life into the rockscape.

The glorious scenery unfolds slowly as the journey proceeds. On the left is **Yewbarrow**, which is not much higher than 2,000ft (600m) but has a 'mountain' appearance. It is a long drag over grassy terrain to get to the summit, which is a vantage point for the really big fells of the dalehead. However, they can also be seen and admired from a car. At centre stage is **Great Gable** (2,949ft/899m), in the form of a rugged pyramid, which confirms everyone's impression of what a mountain should be. Gable's companions are **Kirk Fell** (2,360ft/802m) to the left and **Scafell Pike** (3,206ft/978m). At least, that's how it seems from the floor of Wasdale Valley, though Scafell Pike is the highest peak in England.

TALL STORIES

Wasdale Head is a surprise to those who expect a dale to get narrower and rockier as it comes to its head. For here is a great tract of alluvial soil, thatched in lush green, overlaid by an intricate (and altogether fascinating) pattern of drystone walls. So much stone was cleared from the land

that a lot was simply heaped up and walled around. The **Wasdale Head Inn** has rooms decked with photographs of early climbers. There is also a Ritson Bar, named after Will Ritson, an archetypal dalesman who told 'tall' stories and was fond of saying that Wasdale had the biggest mountain, the deepest lake and the biggest liar – himself (*see page 83*).

Star Attraction
● Viking Cross

VIKING CROSS

On the way from Wasdale, stop in **Gosforth** to see the 14½-ft (4.5-m) carved ★★ **Viking Cross** in the churchyard at St Mary's. Made of red sandstone and somewhat worn after nine centuries of wind and rain, the cross was raised when paganism was giving way to Christianity. Images from Norse mythology and Christian symbolism are portrayed.

ENNERDALE

At **Calder Bridge**, leave the A595 for a hill road to **Ennerdale Bridge**. A stone circle to the right on the moor towards the end of this section is, indeed, a Victorian spoof. A road, ending in a car park, connects the village of Ennerdale Bridge with the end of the public road by **Ennerdale Water**.

Walkers on the **Coast to Coast** route (St Bees to Robin Hoods Bay) and day-trippers with plenty of time and energy walk to the head of Ennerdale. The lower reaches were desecrated by water authority and forestry interests, the period of the massed trees dating from 1927 before the Forestry Commission became 'environmentally friendly'. More recently, the effect has been softened by maturing timber, sensible management and some amenity planting. As the backwoods are left behind, the towering peaks of Great Gable, Kirk Fell, Pillar and Steeple come into view with Hay Stacks rising behind a solitary building, ★ **Black Sail** youth hostel.

The A5086, then the A66, ensure a quick return to Keswick.

Tiny church
The church at Wasdale Head, one of the smallest in England, has timbers said to have come from a shipwrecked vessel. The outline of Nape's Needle, Gable's celebrated rock pinnacle, has been scratched on one of the windows. A conquest of the Needle is obligatory in the career of a Lake District climber. To this end Wasdale attracted a host of Victorian climbers, some of whom exercised on the gable end of a local barn.

Wasdale Church

Map on page 71

8: The Southwest

Grange-over-Sands – Ulverston – Duddon Valley – Wrynose – Grizedale – Cartmel (66 miles/106km)

⚡👁⚡ **Promenading in Grange**
After breakfast in Grange-over-Sands, a stimulating experience is to walk along the promenade, hearing the cries of gulls and other seabirds, or beside the duck-thronged pond in the parkland on land reclaimed when the Furness Railway stabilised the coast with its tracks.

Below: Grange-over-Sands railway station
Bottom: Morecambe Bay

The tide sweeps across Morecambe Bay with the speed of a good horse. It performs pincer movements round the sandbars and spreads itself languidly over the mudflats. In a short time, what had been a damp desert is an arm of the sea, choppy and chilling. Then, with another turn of the tide, the bay is once again what someone called a 'wet Sahara', though this is no desert. On the mudbanks thrive small creatures that sustain dense flocks of wintering birds. Years ago, the bay at low tide would be alive with fisherfolk from the villages who, with horses and carts and tackle, sought cockles, mussels, dabs, flukes and, of course, the famous Morecambe Bay shrimps. North of the bay are limestone hills and beyond them the high fells. A journey in this area is ever-varied. Grange-over-Sands is a good starting point because it grew with tourism and is served by rail and bus. This route runs through Furness, up the glorious Duddon Valley, over the pass into Little Langdale and back via Grizedale Forest and Cartmel Priory.

GRANGE-OVER-SANDS

Grange-over-Sands is on the B5277 – which loops off the A590 halfway between Levens and Newby Bridge. It began as a monastic 'grange' or granary, but a stimulus to the development of Grange took place when it was connected to the rail network in 1857. The Victorian and Edwardian holidaymakers it attracted, and that muddy beach, ensured it would not grow into a major holiday resort. It would remain a place for discerning folk, on whom it thrives today. The architecture of the station, the formal park with its bird-busy lake, the elegant shops with their cast-iron canopy, and the cosy retro tearoom on the promenade, appeal to those who remember a more gracious age. A clock tower makes a brave attempt to give the town a focal point.

Those of an athletic inclination find pleasure in heading upbank from the clock tower, following the signs for ★ **Hampsfell**, with its restored shelter-cum-observation point that offers a fine-weather view of distinction, taking in Ingleborough and other Yorkshire peaks as well as those of the Lake District. A footpath, with views of the bay, leads from Grange to neighbouring **Kents Bank**.

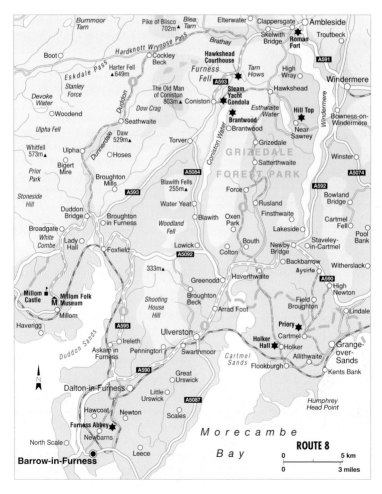

Below and Bottom:
Holker Hall and gardens

Drive to Allithwaite, and from there follow the B5277 westward to **Flookburgh**. The promontory to the left is ★ **Humphrey Head**, the highest point on the west coast between Wales and St Bees Head. Flookburgh, a mile or so inland from Morecambe Bay, was a village of horse-and-cart fisherfolk, who operated on the bay at low tide. Shrimps were caught by a trawl net with a beam. As the beam approached shrimps in one of the channels, they jumped – straight into the net. Cockles by the ton were once transported in sacks from the railway station at Cark. Notice, as you drive towards **Cark**, the next village, that the weathervane on the church is a gilded fish, not a cockerel.

HOLKER HALL

★★ **Holker Hall** (early Jan–mid-Dec, Sun–Fri, hall 10.30am–5.30pm; garden 10am–6pm, 10am–4pm Feb, Nov–Dec) lies just beyond Cark. The splendid home of the Cavendish family dates from 1871, replacing a previous building that was gutted by fire. Red sandstone was used to create a building which has a markedly Elizabethan style. Part of the old 17th-century house remains. It was the home of the Preston family, benefactors of Cartmel Priory. Holker is set in an award-winning garden which, in turn, lies within a deer-haunted park. Joseph Paxton, designer of the Crystal Palace, was invited to plant the 'mon-

key puzzle tree' (Chilean pine). It has reached an enormous size and is pinned down for stability, having once been blown over in a gale. The venerable Holker Lime, listed as one of 50 Great British Trees, is here too. Holker Hall is the venue for a noteworthy annual garden festival. Outbuildings at Holker hold the ★ **Lakeland Motor Museum** (opening hours the same times as Holker Hall). More than 150 classic cars are on view, together with an exhibition on the Campbell water-speed legend and *Bluebird*, a boat with a revolutionary design.

ULVERSTON

The road from Holker unfolds in long straight stretches in an almost flat landscape that consists of sappy grass or indigenous woodland, beloved of naturalists. The road joins the A590, and a turn left leads beside the **Leven Estuary**, where the overflow from Windermere mixes with the salty tide. Continue through Greenodd and on to **Ulverston**, which has a distinctly nautical flavour. The ship canal from the bay was built by John Rennie in 1796, but is now in effect a static water tank for Glaxo-Wellcome. Ulverston has become widely known for its **Laurel and Hardy Museum** (Feb–Dec, daily 10am–4.30pm). Stan Laurel was a native of the town.

SWARTHMOOR AND DALTON

Continue on the A590 to ★ **Swarthmoor** (mid-Mar–mid-Oct, Thur–Fri, Sun guided tours at 2.30pm), an Elizabethan hall of major interest to Quakers. George Fox, founder of the Society of Friends, was a frequent visitor from 1652 when the hall was owned by Judge Thomas Fell and his wife, Margaret. When the judge died in 1658, the immunity he had secured for Quakers lapsed and they were persecuted. Margaret later married George Fox, and both suffered hardship and imprisonment for their beliefs.

At **Dalton-in-Furness**, the so-called castle is a 14th-century tower with monastic links standing

Star Attraction
● Holker Hall

Hoad Hill 'lighthouse'
The limestone 'lighthouse' on Hoad Hill in Ulverston is actually a scaled-down model of the Eddystone lighthouse, built in 1850 in memory of the naval administrator and traveller Sir John Barrow (1764–1848), a native of the town and founder of the Royal Geographical Society. Hoad Hill may be climbed from Ulverston in under half an hour.

The Laurel and Hardy Museum

Map on page 71

in the main street. It was built by the Abbot of Furness when Scottish raiders were troublesome. On the dissolution of Furness Abbey *(see below)*, some of its attractive red sandstone was transported to Dalton to repair the tower, which became a prison and courthouse. Dalton had its economic heyday in the 19th century with the growth of ironstone mining and the lifting of 7 million tons of ore from local mines. Today, the town is more widely known for the **South Lakes Wild Animal Park** (Mar–Oct, daily 10am–5pm, otherwise Sat–Sun 10am–4.30pm. Closed Christmas Day). This is described as Lakeland's only zoological park. Species on show range from free-flying parrots to Sumatran tigers. Recent arrivals include pygmy hippos and black-footed penguins.

Below: Furness train times
Bottom: arched cloister at Furness Abbey

FURNESS ABBEY

Not far from Dalton, to the left of the A590 and on the edge of mighty Barrow, a short, constricted road leads under a monastic arch to the outstanding remains of ★★★ **Furness Abbey** (Easter–Nov daily, Nov–Easter Wed–Sun). Originally founded in 1127 by monks of the Order of Savigny, Furness later joined the Cistercians and became one of the richest abbeys in the land. The area became known as the Vale of Deadly Nightshade because of the profusion of those plants. The Abbey's extensive remains, on a 73-acre (30-hectare) site,

are breathtaking. Rose-red sandstone stands out against the green of well-manicured lawns. The nave and transepts date from the 12th century, the massive west tower from the 15th century. **The Dock Museum**, signposted in Barrow (Tues–Sun, Mon in high summer), is built over an original Victorian graving dock.

Star Attraction
● **Furness Abbey**

BROUGHTON AND MILLOM

The A595 turns northwards, with a gleam from the Duddon estuary to the west. Drive around the estuary to **Broughton-in-Furness** just off the A595. The name Broughton is Old English and means a farmstead or village by a stream. Now there is a settlement with a market square, overlooked by fine buildings, shadowed by trees and with a set of stocks as a reminder of an old-time punishment.

Carry on around the side of the estuary and the goose-frequented marshes, beneath the brooding **Black Combe**, to the quaint little Victorian town of ★ **Millom**, a child of the Furness ironstone boom and the home of Norman Nicholson (1914–87), a poet in the Wordsworthian tradition. His bust bedecks the library, and he is deemed important enough to warrant a section to himself in the adjacent folk museum. Less than a mile from the town of Millom, beside the A5093, are **Millom Castle** (a pele tower) and a restored 13th-century **church** that hint at the pre-industrialised feel of the area

DUDDON VALLEY

Backtrack along the A595, but turn left just before the narrow bridge spanning the **River Duddon**, and enter the **Duddon Valley**. The road runs high, offering views across wooded hills, which in the days of Furness Abbey provided timber for the making of charcoal and in the 18th century supplied fuel for an early **forge**, the substantial remains of which, not far from Duddon Bridge, are preserved. The iron ore was brought up the Duddon, and the forge operated using charcoal made from local woodland, which was clear-felled

Birks Bridge
The most attractive part of Duddon Valley is where Birks Bridge, a single span across a gorge, enables people to pass dryshod over the swirling river. The pools have a dark green hue. Rowans (mountain ash) have rooted among the rocks. The big conifer forest to the west of the river dates back 60 years to when the Forestry Commission planted dense ranks of alien spruce. The passing years have brought some welcome changes. There are now picnic areas and other facilities for public use.

The Duddon idyll

Map on page 71

and burnt slowly in 'pits'. Wordsworth wrote a sequence of 35 sonnets about the River Duddon, describing it as 'majestic' and, at Duddon Bridge, making 'radiant progress towards the deep'.

The Duddon frolics between jumbled boulders and the dried fronds of bracken, providing perfect picnic areas, though being secluded the valley does not attract a great many visitors. Humans have lived in these parts for several thousand years, judging by sepulchral mounds on the flanking hills from which have been taken calcified bones.

Kirk of Ulpha

Situated between Duddon Bridge and Seathwaite, the village of Ulpha has a little gem of a church – Wordsworth's 'Kirk of Ulpha' – perched on a knoll beside the road and dedicated to St John the Baptist. The font is ancient, and the altar is fashioned from the wood of a fruit tree. Ulpha, who gave his name to the main settlement, is said to have been the son of Evard. He received the manor when the land was re-apportioned following the Norman Conquest.

SEATHWAITE

The hamlet of **Seathwaite** (a Norse name derived from 'clearing of the shieling', a summer pasture) has an inn. Robert Walker (1709–1802), who was curate at Seathwaite for well over 60 years, became known as Wonderful Walker because of his thrift and industry. Although on a stipend of only a few pounds a year, he had managed to accrue £2,000 by the time he died at the age of 92. His wife, who was equally thrifty, died in the same year. The curate is commemorated by a plaque in the local church.

GRIZEDALE FOREST

At **Cockley Beck**, those wishing to test their motoring skills on **Hardknott Pass** *(see page 66)*

Cartmel Village Square

cross the bridge over the Duddon. Otherwise keep straight ahead along **Wrynose Bottom**, source of the Duddon. Three Shires Stone offers a chance to park and stretch the legs before the steep descent into Little Langdale, having exchanged the Duddon for the Brathay (*see pages 37 and 67*).

Join the A593 and go south to **Coniston**, following the B5285 to Hawkshead (*see page 40*). Just south of the village is a turning on the right to ★★ **Grizedale Forest**, developed on an 8,000-acre (3,200-hectare) estate purchased by the Forestry Commission in 1937. During World War II, Grizedale Hall was used to house prisoners. In the post-war period, the Commission pioneered the concept of a commercial forest to which the public is granted access in order to learn about the countryside and walk along waymarked paths, adorned by fascinating sculptures, the work of young artists. From the deer museum, opened in 1956, has developed a visitor centre, forest shop, exhibition and tearoom. Also within the forest is **Go Ape!** (Mar–Oct) a high-ropes aerial adventure course through the tree tops.

CARTMEL

Continue to **Satterthwaite**, **Rusland**, **Booth** and the A590, where you turn left through Backbarrow and Newby Bridge to a right-hand turning for **Cartmel**. You'll notice, as the village comes into view, the upstanding and carefully preserved ★★ **Priory**, with the curious diagonal extension to its central tower.

The main fabric is original, created in 1188. A mother and son who drowned while crossing Morecambe Bay sands by the old low-tide route from Hest Bank are buried next to the font.

Elsewhere in the village is the well-preserved monastic gatehouse, which was in use from 1624 until 1790 as a grammar school. It now belongs to the National Trust and is a **Village Heritage Centre** (Easter–end-October, Tues–Sun 10am-4pm, winter Sat–Sun only). **Cartmel Races** take place in an attractive parkland area.

Grange-over-Sands lies just over the hill.

Star Attractions
- **Grizedale Forest**
- **Cartmel Priory**

Below: Cartmel Priory
Bottom: Grizedale Forest sculpture

The Historic Landscape

Our knowledge of early life in the Lake District was transformed in 1947 by the discovery of pieces of chipped volcanic rock on the 2,000-ft (600-m) scree slope of Pike o'Stickle at the head of Great Langdale *(see page 66)*. This proved to be the site of a **prehistoric axe-factory**, the first major Lake District industry, operating in Neolithic times, some 4,000 years ago.

Until this find, it had been thought that penetration of Central Lakeland had occurred much later. At Pike o'Stickle, and various other places in the high fell country, pieces of tuff, a particularly hard rock, were 'roughed out' with hammers made of granite. Then (it is theorised) they were taken to the coastal strip for final shaping. Langdale rock was traded throughout the country. The Great Cumbrian Axe was set to work to thin out the old forest, which extended far up the hillsides.

The Mesolithic folk had been hunters, their dreams haunted by such images as the red deer. In Neolithic times, people were clothing themselves with wool from the crag sheep, and burial urns were being used.

When the Romans swept north in the first century AD, the Lake District (like most of the North Country) was tenanted by a tribe known as the Brigantes. The most memorable of the ancient sites of the Lake District is that of a **Roman fort** beside Hardknott Pass *(see page 66)*. It stood beside a road connecting Ambleside with the natural harbour at Ravenglass. The appreciable remains of the fort are on a spur of land at an elevation of 800ft (244m). Archaeologists affirm that the builders of this fort came from the Balkans.

ARCHITECTURE

Pele towers, three storeys high and considered impregnable, are distinctive early stone structures, now (in most cases) forming the core of much larger buildings, as at Levens Hall, Sizergh Castle *(see page 20)* and Kentmere Hall.

Ancient Monuments
Spectacular stone circles were raised in the late Neolithic and the early Bronze Age, the most notable being at Castlerigg, near Keswick *(see page 45)*. Much smaller, but impressive in its broad moorland setting, is the Cockpit on Askham Moor. It's an easy walk from the village, near Penrith, to the moor, where the visual remains of ancient peoples are to be seen everywhere.

*Opposite:
Sizergh Castle
Below: Castlerigg
stone circle*

At Burneside *(see page 22)* the pele tower, adjacent to a farmhouse, is partly ruined and gives an insight into the fine details of its construction. Pele towers date from the 14th century, when local people sought protection from repetitive Scottish raids.

The circular chimneys so highly praised by Wordsworth were not so much for show as the best way of using irregular stones. Large houses of early date include Coniston Hall, with its cluster of circular chimneys above open hearths (to be seen after a short walk from the *Gondola*'s pier at Coniston Water, *see page 38*).

In the 17th century, with the Border troubles over and Lakeland families having security of tenure, there was a widespread reconstruction of farmhouses. A typical 17th-century Lakeland farm was built of stone and slate wrenched from quarries near at hand, with small windows and a stout porch to protect the front door from the searching wind. Some, as at Hartsop *(see page 32)* and Yew Tree Farm near Coniston have 'spinning galleries'.

Most of the dalehead farms are now owned by the National Trust. An outstanding example of a Lakeland yeoman's home is Townend at Troutbeck *(see page 33)*.

> **In the vernacular**
> There is a roughness about many farmhouses that reflects the unsuitability of local stone, but the builders did their best. Every dale has fine examples of this vernacular architecture.

Below: Hartsop farmhouse with spinning gallery
Bottom: Details and decoration

DISTINCTIVE FORMS

Apart from the typical Lakeland farms and cottages constructed, sometimes with difficulty, from the native stone and slate, the Lake District was the setting for some distinctive architectural forms imposed on it by outsiders and usually criticised by the neighbours for doubtful, if not bad, taste. One such structure is the Round House on Belle Island, Windermere, built on a whim by Mr English in 1774, badly damaged by fire in recent times and now in the course of reconstruction.

The most famous 'odd' building in the Lake District must be the Bridge House, sitting over a stream in Ambleside, which many people falsely claim was built by a Scotsman who wanted to avoid paying ground rent *(see page 26)*.

LITERATURE

Lakeland literature is enlivened by the writings of **Dorothy** and **William Wordsworth**, brother and sister, who were born at Cockermouth, sojourned for a while in the South and returned to live in the Lake District, at Dove Cottage, Grasmere, in 1799. Dorothy's prose work is best seen in her *Journal*. Apart from his immense output of verse, William wrote a perceptive guide book to the area. Wordsworth and his friends, including **Samuel Taylor Coleridge**, **Robert Southey** and **Thomas De Quincey**, became known as the Lake Poets. Southey, who settled for a while in Keswick, was appointed Poet Laureate in 1813.

The Lake District was home for an appreciable period to **John Ruskin** (at Brantwood, above Coniston Water), **Hugh Walpole** (at Brackenburn, near Grange-in-Borrowdale), **Arthur Ransome** (who drew partly on memories of childhood holidays at Nibthwaite, by Coniston Water for his *Swallows and Amazons* and many other books) and **Beatrix Potter** (Sawrey, near Hawkshead).

Below: William Wordsworth
Bottom: Beatrix Potter
Museum, Hawkshead

A SENSE OF PLACE

A stylish writer in prose and verse who drew much of his creative strength from contemplation of the basic rocks of the Lake District and life in his native, industrialised Millom, was

Norman Nicholson. Lakeland novels were produced by **Graham Sutton**, who lived near Keswick. In his classic *Fell Days*, he reproduced his hilarious short story, 'The Man Who Broke the Needle', a reference to the celebrated 'stack' on the flanks of Great Gable. A climber who thought he had broken it by dislodging the piece at the top was relieved to find he was dreaming while languishing in his dentist's chair. The needle had broken.

Below: dressed for the Rushbearing
Bottom: Tent Lodge, by Coniston Water painted by J.M.W. Turner

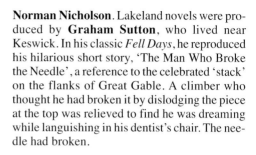

ART

To list the artists who have been inspired by the Lake District would be to risk writer's cramp. They include the incomparable **J.M.W. Turner**, who on a tour in 1797, with the Romantic Age in full swing, produced *Morning amongst the Coniston Fells* (Tate Britain, London). Engravings and drawings in vast numbers were produced commercially by **William Green**, who settled in Ambleside a few years later. **John Constable**, on a single visit (in 1806) made many sketches and watercolours but later confessed he had found the mountains oppressive.

Of modern artists, **Delmar Banner** had a genius for presenting Lakeland fells wrapped in cloud. A special tribute should be paid to the Cooper family. At the Heaton Cooper Studio in

Grasmere is a permanent exhibition of water-colours and a large collection of colour repro-ductions of the Lake District by **W. Heaton Cooper** (1903–95) and his father, **A. Heaton Cooper** (1863–1929).

FESTIVALS AND FOLKLORE

For centuries, the Lake District proper was a secluded, little-known corner of England, too close to the Scottish border for comfort, and keeping largely to itself. Sheep farming was a primary activity, and entertainment was homespun. Lake-landers developed a love of **sport**, **song** and **dance** (to the strains of fiddle or accordion). Vital events such as the **shepherds' meet**, when stray sheep from the 'gathering' were returned to their right-ful owners, saw an explosion of local feeling in **fox-hunting** and, later, **hound-trailing**. At the end of the day, the Cumbrian dalesman resorted to hard drinking, lusty singing, and much eating of **tatie pot** (a local meat and potato stew).

  Cumberland and Westmorland wrestling, which is claimed to be the type used when Jacob wrestled with the Angel, demands brains as well as brawn and began with school lads 'takking 'od' (taking hold) on a village green. Such wrestling became respectable when it was to be seen at the **Grasmere Sports**, held in August, which was patronised by Lord Lonsdale from Lowther Park. Among the more bizarre forms of expression which once was in vogue and now survives at **Egremont** was **gurning** (pulling the funniest face) through a **braffin** (horse-collar). A novel event in Santon Bridge, attended by much drink-ing and hilarity, is a competition to find **t'biggest liar**, thus keeping alive a tradition dating back to Will Ritson, of **Wasdale Head**, a teller of out-rageous tales.

  The church has conserved much of the local culture. The **Rushbearing** dates back to the days when churches had earthen floors and on a spec-ified day freshly cut rushes were spread on the ground. Rushbearings at Ambleside and Gras-mere attract large crowds.

Festival Highlights
Contact Tourist Information at Cumbrian Tourist Board 01539 822222 for precise dates.

Cartmel Races: late spring and late summer, Bank Holidays, Saturday and Monday. Steeplechasing.

Brathay Windermere Marathon: thrid Sunday in May.

Appleby Horse Fair: in early June. Fair Hill near Appleby. One of the country's largest gatherings of Romany families, some with vardos (horse-drawn caravans).

Rushbearing: Ambleside – first Sat-urday in July; Grasmere – Saturday nearest 5 August. Procession to church, singing of a special Rush-bearing hymn.

Penrith Agricultural Show: late July. An extensive range of livestock, rural crafts, and food. Kicks off with a Grand Parade

Maryport Blues Festival: late July. With many top international per-formers.

Borrowdale Shepherds' Meet and Show: mid-September.

Bowness Theatre Festival & Film: late September.

World's Biggest Liar Competi-tion: mid-November. Bridge Inn, Santon Bridge near Eskdale.

Kendal Mountain Film Festival: November. International showcase for mountain films and photographs.

Wasdale Head Shepherds' Meet: second Saturday in October.

FOOD AND DRINK

Traditionally, it was **poddish** (porridge) for breakfast. This was served so thick that a mouse might walk dryshod across it. Working on the principle that *it's your stomach 'at 'ods your back up*, the Lakeland-born dined heartily on **tatie pot**, a glorious mixture of mutton or lamb, black pudding and potatoes, frequently served as a supper during some hectic round of dancing.

MEAT AND FISH
The lile **Herdwick**, as the native sheep was called, might have poor quality wool but its meat was regarded as mutton fit for a king. **Cumberland sausage** is produced in a large herby coil, and it traditionally has good lumps of fat within to help with the cooking. Variations on the theme are smoked sausages made of wild boar and venison. Cumberland cured gammon steak is another delicacy to ask about. Curiously, when **Windermere char** (a deepwater fish) are offered for sale in the Bowness area, it is the butcher, not the fishmonger, who stocks it, and is usually bought up by the big hotels.

CAKES AND ALE
At Grasmere, the smell of fresh gingerbread has flavoured the air for 140 years, leading visitors to the **Gingerbread Shop**, tucked away in a corner of St Oswald's churchyard. Another spicy traditional treat is **Westmorland pepper cake**. Jennings Brewery at Cockermouth has been producing **ale** since 1828 and has daily tours of their Castle Brewery. Telephone 0845 129 7185 for times and availability. Visitors see the processes involved and are invited to sample the end result.

Left: a famous product of Kendal

RESTAURANT AND TEAROOM SELECTION
The following is a selection of recommended restaurants in the main centres of the Lake District. Tearooms are included because of the long association with local tourism. They are listed according to three price categories: **£££** = expensive; **££** = moderate; **£** = inexpensive.

Ambleside
The Drunken Duck, Barngates, tel: 015394 36347. Award-winning gastro pub serving its own ales. **££**
The Glass House Restaurant, Rydal Road, tel: 015394 32137. A 15th-century cloth mill, situated behind the famous Bridge House. Modern European and traditional British food. **£**
Lucy's on a Plate, Compston Road, tel: 015394 31191. Popular café with fireplace, walled garden and adjoining delicatessen. **£**
Zeffirellis, Compston Road, tel: 015394 33845. Warm and stylish wholefood restaurant with a pleasant buzz. There is also a café, a jazz bar and a four-screen cinema . The meal-cinema package offers good value. **£**

Bowness
The Porthole, 3 Ash Street, tel: 015394 42793. A converted 17th-century cottage with dining either

---

Lyth Valley Damsons
September is the best time to tour the Lyth Valley (southeast of Bowness) for damsons. Roadside stalls and local shops usually have a good supply, though in some years fruit is scarce. Contact the Westmorland Damson Association on tel: 015395 68246 or visit www.lythsdamsons.org.uk for more information.

downstairs or at the front of the restaurant. Bar, Italian patio, and a balcony upstairs. Closed Tuesday. **££**

Carlisle

Garden Restaurant, Tullie House Museum and Art Gallery, tel: 01228 534781. Daily specials, a fresh salad bar and home-baked treats. **£**

Cartmel

L'Enclume, Cavendish Street, tel: 015395 36362. Michelin-starred modern French cuisine in a stylishly converted blacksmith's workshop. **£££**
Cavendish Arms Hotel, Cavendish Street, tel: 01539536240. A 16th-century coaching inn with a high reputation for its catering. **££**

Coniston

Jumping Jenny, tel: 015394 41715. Coffees, teas and lunches at Brantwood, Ruskin's old home, east of Coniston Water. Magnificent Coniston views from the terrace. Reached by road or Coniston Launch. **£**

Crosthwaite

The Punch Bowl Inn, tel: 015395 68237. A 17th-century inn with good

The Glass House, Ambleside

food, traditional ales and an extensive list of wines by the glass. **£**

Eskdale

Bower House Inn, Holmbrook, tel: 019467 23244. Another fine old inn. Log fires, real ale, tatie pot and other traditional fare. **£**
The Woolpack Inn, Boot, tel: 019467 23230. Well-known hostelry in western Lake District. Good food with a selection of real ale. **£**

Glenridding

Fellbites, Croft House, tel: 017684 82781. Lakeland specialities such as Ullswater trout. **£**

Grange-in-Borrowdale

The Borrowdale Gates Country House Hotel, tel: 017687 77204. Fine food each evening cooked by the chef-patron. Light lunches and afternoon teas in the lounges. **££**

Grasmere

Villa Colombina Dove Cottage Restaurant, tel: 015394 35268. Near the famous home of William Wordsworth. Open all day. **£**
The Jumble Room, Langdale Road, tel: 015394 35188. A selection of dishes from around the world, in comfortable surroundings. **££**

Hawkshead

Queen's Head Hotel, Main Street, tel: 015394 36271. Traditional English cuisine served in a mellow, wood-panelled dining room. **£**

Kendal

Abbot Art Gallery, near the church, free parking for visitors, tel: 01539 722464. Lunch and refreshments in the coffee shop. **£**

Low Sizergh Barn Farm Shop and Tearoom, Low Sizergh Farm, beside the Kendal by-pass, tel: 01539 560426. 17th-century stone barn, with farm shop selling local produce. The rustic tearoom overlooks the milking parlour, where cows are milked at about 3.30pm every day. **££**

The Green Room, The Brewery Art Centre, tel: 01539 725133. Lunch may be taken on the garden patio. In the evening, the speciality items are bistro-style dishes and cinema suppers (two-course meal plus cinema ticket). **£**

Keswick

Highfield Hotel Restaurant, The Heads, tel: 017687 72508. Imaginative modern European cuisine and wonderful views. Menu changes daily. **££**

Lairbeck Hotel, Vicarage Hill, tel: 017687 73373. Fresh food with an emphasis on local produce. **££**

The Rembrandt Restaurant, Station Street, tel: 017687 72008. Unstinting portions of traditional food, including home-made sweets. **£**

The Old Sawmill Tearoom, 3½ miles (5km) north of Keswick on the A591 opposite Mirehouse, tel: 017687 74317. Noted for its local-style home cooking and fresh baked goods. **£**

Little Salkeld, nr Penrith

Watermill Tearoom, tel: 01768 881523. Teas, coffees and baked goods produced entirely from organic flours milled on the premises. Mill tours. **£**

Local food trails
Discover the finest organic produce in Cumbria and visit the apple orchards and local breweries. Food-themed trail leaflets exploring the diversity of local produce include Ale Trail, Apple Appeal, A Taste of Honey, Damson Valleys, Organic Origins, and Sausage Secrets. Available from Tourist Information Centres.

Newby Bridge nr Ulverston

Swan Hotel, tel: 015395 31681. Beside the Leven, the overflow of Windermere. Dine at Revells Restaurant or the less formal Mailcoach Brasserie. Licensed bars. **££**

Skelwith Bridge

Chesters Café by the River, shares premises with Touchstone Interiors beside the Ambleside–Coniston road at the junction to Great Langdale, tel: 015394 32553. Delicious home-made cakes and lunches on the River Brathay. **£**

Whitehaven

The Waterfront, tel: 01946 691130. Harbourside bar and restaurant with friendly service and a variety of daily specials. **£**

Windermere

Miller Howe, Rayrigg Road, tel: 015394 42536. For gourmets who enjoy immaculate service. **£££**

The Queen's Head Hotel, Troutbeck, tel: 015394 32174. Oak beams, flag floor, log fire. Open all year. **££**

Brockhole Visitor Centre, National Park between Windermere and Ambleside. Café serving traditional Cumbrian recipes. Open April to October. **£**

Gilpin Lodge, tel: 015394 88818. Excellent food featuring local produce. Substantial afternoon teas.

ACTIVE HOLIDAYS

Variations on the 'activity' theme in an area of mountains, crags and lakes are limitless. Information is available from the Tourist Board, or by visiting www.lakedistrictoutdoors.co.uk. Lakeland offers walking and weaving, pony trekking and painting, quilting or canoeing, paragliding, golfing, mountain biking, trekking, angling and much more.

WALKING

The most common form of recreation in the Lake District is walking, and the best-known handbooks for walkers are the Pictorial Guides of Alfred Wainwright. The original edition is now somewhat out of date but has retained its charm. A podcast has recently been produced by Cumbria Tourism giving fans a chance to 'walk with Wainwright' on Helm Crag. This free download is available to those with iPods on www.golakes.co.uk/wainwrightpodcast.

The shelves of Lake District bookshops are crammed with guide books, most of which describe walking circular routes. The Ordnance Survey maps are the most detailed. The Lake District National Park organises walks for visitors, details being given in their free newspaper, which is available at any Information Centre. Information Centres stock local maps showing walks suitable for people with disabilities.

A good short walk (about 2½ hours) is round **Buttermere**, one of the quieter lakes, starting at a car park in the village. The route is suitable for visitors in wheelchairs. Somewhat longer is the circumnavigation of **Grasmere** and **Rydal**, beginning at one of the car parks of Grasmere and walking on a well-beaten path to the west of the lakes, one stretch of the way being the celebrated **Loughrigg**

Terrace. Return to Grasmere on a hillside path which begins near Rydal Mount *(see page 50)*.

Among the popular but more exacting hill walks of the Lake District is a circuit taking in the **Langdale Pikes**, beginning and ending at the Dungeon Ghyll car park at the head of Great Langdale. In the east of the region, the summit of **Helvellyn** can be approached from either Thirlmere or Ullswater, a possible route from the latter being up the magnificent Striding Edge (in calm and non-slippery conditions).

In Central Lakeland, **Great Gable** can be ascended from Honister Pass, Styhead Tarn from the head of Borrowdale or Wasdale Head. Wasdale Head is the most popular departure point for those wishing to conquer **Scafell Pike**. The southern fells are dominated by **Coniston Old Man**, and **Skiddaw** looms over to the north. Skiddaw's summit is an easy hike from Millbeck, to the north of Keswick.

BIRDWATCHING

The diverse Lakeland environment hosts a wide range of birdlife. Buz-

Climbing
Although there is a wide range of climbs in the Lake District, this is not a sport that can be undertaken casually. Many young people learn the techniques through Outward Bound or Field Centres. Wasdale is a favourite of many an experienced climber. Langdale, Coniston and Pillar rocks are durable and popular. Climbers might be seen on crags near the Jaws of Borrowdale, and there are some nursery pitches not far from the Bowder Stone. Shops selling outdoor garb usually have a stock of climbing books.

zards, ravens and peregrines inhabit the higher elevations throughout the year, while numerous species of waterfowl populate the fresh water lagoons, salt marshes and mudflats. Spring is the best time to spot migratory species in the lower woodland slopes and valleys.

Wild ospreys have returned to England; the first chicks for more than 150 years hatched in Cumbria in 2004. Ospreys can be seen at Thornthwaite Forest in the Keswick district.

CYCLING AND PONY TREKKING

There has been a rapid increase in the number of mountain bikers using the Lake District. It is possible to hire a mountain bike (all-terrain bicycle or ATB) in Ambleside, Coniston, Grizedale, Kendal, Keswick and Windermere. The Cumbria Cycle Way of 280 miles (450km) is a circular, waymarked route for which quiet country roads were chosen.

The marks of cycle tyres are now seen near the imprint of walking boots and the shoes of the stocky pony used for trekking. Some of the ponies are of the fell breed, which has ranged the Lake District fells for centuries.

One of the most popular ways to get around

WATER SPORTS

Water sports are well-catered for around Windermere, including windsurfing and children's water-skiing. Because of new speed restrictions (10 mph/16 kph) on power boats, some water sports are not permissable.

FISHING

Anglers need a North West Water Authority rod licence (inquire at any tackle shop or visit www.environment-agency.gov.uk/subjects/fish) plus a fishing permit. Esthwaite Water is the region's top trout lake. Contact Esthwaite Water Trout Fishery, tel: 015394 36541 for information. Another useful website is www.lakedistrictfishing.net.

GOLF

Golf flourishes on more than 20 good-sized courses ranging from pay-and-play to championship links. Day tickets are available. Visit the Cumbria Union of Golf website www.cumbria-golf-union.org.uk for more information.

OTHER SPORTS

Unusual ways of tuning up the body as well as the mind include gorge-scrambling, aquasailing and (at Flookburgh) parachuting. There are sports centres at Kendal, Keswick, Cockermouth and Whitehaven.

PRACTICAL INFORMATION

Getting There

BY TRAIN

Virgin trains from London to Oxenholme (connecting with a local service to Windermere) take 3 hours and 1½ hours from Edinburgh to Carlisle – a little longer to Penrith; visit www.virgintrains.com. From Yorkshire, the Settle–Carlisle railway is served by Northern Rail diesel multiple units. Northern Rail also runs the Scenic Cumbria Coast Line connecting Barrow-in-Furness, Whitehaven and Carlisle. The Furness Line from Lancaster connects Grange-over-Sands, Cartmel and Barrow-in-Furness. Details of rail services are available from any railway station or tel: National Rail Enquiries 08457 484 950 or visit www.nationalrail.co.uk

BY ROAD

The Lake District is about 5½ hours from London by road, using the motorway system. The M6 gives quick access to the Lake District, with points of exit at Lancaster, the Kendal bypass, Shap and Penrith. By road from Dover to Windermere is 353 miles (570km); from the North Sea ferry at Hull to Windermere is 139 miles (224km).

BY AIR

Overseas visitors find Manchester Airport most convenient for Cumbria. Manchester is adjacent to the M6, which runs along the eastern fringe of the Lake District. Trains depart from the airport railway station to Barrow-in-Furness, Windermere, Penrith and Carlisle. Teesside, Leeds/Bradford, Newcastle and Blackpool airports are also within striking distance.

BY COACH

National Express runs the Express Rapide service from London to Kendal. For details of this and other coach services to the area tel: 0871 200 2233, or visit www.traveline.org.uk

Getting Around

For details of bus and rail services throughout Cumbria, contact Traveline on 0871 200 2233 or consult the nearest Tourist Information Centre (*see pages 91–2*).

BY TRAIN

The 72-mile (116-km) Settle–Carlisle line is of high scenic interest, travelling through the north–south valleys of the Ribble and Eden between the Lakeland fells and the Pennines with high country in between that features huge viaducts and long tunnels. Equally impressive is the system which takes in the Cumbrian coast, from Lancaster or Barrow-in-Furness to Carlisle. Starting from Lancaster allows a return from Carlisle to Lancaster by InterCity over Shap Fell and through the Lune Gorge.

Ravenglass and Eskdale Railway, nicknamed Ratty, is England's oldest narrow-gauge steam railway. It operates over 7 miles (11km) of track through arresting scenery. For more information, tel: 01229 717171 or visit www.ravenglass-railway.co.uk

Lakeside & Haverthwaite Railway connects at Lakeside, Windermere, with a 'steamer' voyage to Bowness

---

♙ Footloose and Car Free
Car-free day itineraries using a combination of steam trains, boats, buses, bicycles and short walks are available from Tourist Information Centres. A 'CarFree Care-Free' ticket allows discounted transport and entry to many of the attractions along the way.

and Waterhead. At Haverthwaite, beside the A590, is a car park, refreshment room, shop and display of locomotives. For an informative leaflet, with details of times and main line savings, tel: 015395 31594.

BY CAR

The car is the handiest form of transport in the Lakes, but at peak times it causes acute congestion, and there are calls from preservation groups for controls in the National Park. Parking may be difficult at the height of the season. Most car parks now have pay-and-display facilities The machines do not give change, so carry a variety of coins. Or, in the case of National Park car parks, enquire about season tickets. Most of the main centres , such as Windermere and Ambleside, have one-way traffic systems in operation. This also applies to the main area of the car parks at Bowness Bay.

BY BUS

The main bus company is Stagecoach. Caldbeck Rambler service from Keswick calls at villages in the Northern Fells. To check bus availability call Traveline 0871 200 2233.

BY BOAT

Hundreds of boats are to be seen on Windermere at the height of the season. Windermere Lake Cruises, operating from Lakeside, maintains a year-round service using traditional 'steamers', *Swan*, *Teal* and *Tern*, from Ambleside, Bowness and Lakeside, including a summer connection with the Lakeside & Haverthwaite Steam Railway and the National Park Visitor Centre at Brockhole. For information, contact Windermere Lake Cruises on: 015395 31188. All-weather motor cruisers operate trips from Bowness Bay.

On Derwentwater, near Keswick, some motor launches operate to a timetable, maintaining a valuable transport link with piers around the lake. The National Trust steam yacht *Gondola*, launched in 1859, sails to a timetable on Coniston Water, tel: 015394 41288.

Ullswater Steamers (*Raven, Lady of the Lake, Lady Dorothy,* and *Lady Wakefield*) runs services according to the season between Glenridding, Howtown and Pooley Bridge and 1-hour cruises from Glenridding. Refreshments and bars on board. Enquiries at Glenridding Pier, tel: 017684 82229.

IN A GUIDED PARTY

Mountain Goat Tours, Victoria Street, Windermere, tel: 015394 45161. Mini-coaches with panoramic windows. Lakeland Safari, 23 Fisherbeck Park, Ambleside, tel: 015394 33904. Various tours in six-seater vehicles. Lakes Supertours, 1 High Street, Windermere, tel: 015394 88133. Small informal groups in mini-coaches. Tours are also arranged by Browns of Ambleside, a long-established firm.

Facts for the Visitor

TOURIST INFORMATION CENTRES

The Cumbria Tourist Board has its headquarters at Ashleigh, Holly Road, Windermere LA23 2AQ, tel: 015398 22222 fax: 015398 250794. The following centres have verbal and printed information.

Ambleside, Central Buildings, Market Cross, tel: 015394 32582; **Barrow-in-Furness**, Forum 28, Duke Street, tel: 01229 820 000; **Bowness-on-Windermere**, Glebe Road, tel: 015394 42895; **Cockermouth**, Town Hall, Market Street, tel: 01900 822634; **Coniston**, Ruskin Avenue, tel: 015394 41533; **Grange-over-Sands**, Victoria

Hall, Main Street, tel: 015395 34026; **Kendal**, Town Hall, Highgate, tel: 01539 725758; **Keswick**, Moot Hall, Market Square, tel: 017687 72645; **Maryport**, Maryport Town Hall, 1 Senhouse Street, tel: 01900 813738; **Penrith**, Robinson's School, Middlegate, tel: 01768 867466; **Ulverston**, Coronation Hall, County Square, tel: 01229 587120; **Whitehaven**, Market Hall, Market Place, tel: 01946 852939; **Windermere**, Victoria Street, tel: 015394 46499.

> **Medical assistance**
> Nationals of the European Union are entitled to free medical treatment in any part of the UK. Some other countries also have reciprocal arrangements for free treatment. However, most visitors from abroad have to pay for medical and dental treatment and should ensure that they have adequate health insurance. Furness General Hospital in Barrow-in-Furness has a 24-hour accident and emergency unit, and Westmorland General Hospital in Kendal has an accident and minor emergency unit.

Children

Facilities range from theme attractions, such as those associated with **Beatrix Potter**, and parks, such as **Grizedale Forest**, to adventurous activity like **camping** and **canoeing**, as written about so evocatively in the 1930s and '40s by Arthur Ransome in the adventures *Swallows and Amazons* (expert tuition is available in most areas).

Brockhole Visitor Centre (tel: 015394 46601) has special arrangements for children, with hands-on possibilities. The adventure playground is varied and imaginative. Older children may like to try their hand at **drystone walling**.

At the **World of Beatrix Potter** (tel: 015394 88444), in Bowness, a young visitor might explore Mr McGregor's garden and Mrs Tiggy-Winkle's kitchen (all year, except Christmas Day and early January).

At Lowther, 4 miles (6.5km) south of Penrith on the A6, is **Lakeland Bird of Prey Centre** (tel: 01931 712746). Birds are flown daily. Visitors who wander around see hawks, eagles and owls at close quarters.

Keswick has for long been a famous place for pencil-making. How the industry came into existence, and how pencils are made, can be seen at the \ **Pencil Museum** (tel: 017687 73626) adjacent to the works. Years ago, graphite mined at the head of Borrowdale was used for pencil-making. See the longest pencil in the world (7.91m/25ft 11½ inches).

A few miles north of Keswick, on the A591, children can let off steam in the four woodland adventure playgrounds at **Mirehouse** (tel: 017687 72287).

Young people who enjoy visiting remoter country might be taken to the head of **Borrowdale**, where the evidence of mining is still to be seen on the fellside. (Stay above ground!)

Pony trekking is an adventurous way of seeing the country. The ponies follow the green tracks on which, years ago, packhorse trains operated, moving goods from one settlement to another and carrying wool into Kendal for processing (Lakeland Pony Trekking, tel: 015394 31999). Children will also enjoy the novelty of **Lakeland Llama Treks** (tel: 0870 7707175).

Another form of transport popular with children is the **Ravenglass and Eskdale Railway** (tel: 01229 717171). Nearby, on the A595, 'Haunted' **Muncaster Castle** (tel: 01229 717614) has the World Owl Centre with daily flyings on the castle lawn, and also the Meadow Vole maze, specially designed for children.

ACCOMMODATION

Lake District accommodation is listed in a free guide available from Information Centres or the Cumbrian Tourist Board *(see pages 91–2)*. Assistance with booking is available on the booking hotline: 0845 450 1199. A price guide for the basic cost for one person sharing a twin/double room is shown here with pound symbols: **£££** is over £70, **££** is £40–70 and **£** is under £40

Ambleside

Waterhead Hotel, Lake Road, tel: 015394 32566; www.elh.co.uk Well-established, recently modernised luxury town house hotel in a prime lakeside position. Lake views from all guest rooms. Good food. **££**

Wateredge Inn, Borrans Road, Waterhead Bay, tel: 015394 32332; www.wateredgeinn.co.uk Family-run hotel with pleasant gardens down to the lake. **££**

Cote How Country Guest House, Rydal, tel: 015394 32765; www.cote-how.co.uk A very pretty guesthouse and organic tearooom, ideal for walkers and for those seeking peace and quiet (no TVs). Friendly, helpful hosts. **££**

Brantfell, Rothay Road, tel: 015394 32239. Victorian House with views; traditional and vegetarian food. **£**

Fisherbeck Hotel, Lake Road, tel: 015394 33215; www.fisherbeckhotel.co.uk Family-run hotel with views over Lake Windermere from most rooms. No children under 7. Restaurant and pretty garden. **£**

Borrowdale

Borrowdale Gates, tel: 017687 77204; www.borrowdale-gates.com Large Victorian Lakeland house with panoramic views and excellent food. **£££**

Hazel Bank Country House, Rosthwaite, tel: 017687 77248; www.hazelbankhotel.co.uk Highly commended. Non-smoking. No pets. **££**

Seatoller House, tel: 017687 77218; www.seatollerhouse.co.uk Informal and special. Good food. **£**

Cartmel

Aynsome Manor Hotel, tel: 015395 36653; www.aynsomemanorhotel.co.uk Sixteenth-century manor in the Vale of Cartmel, off the tourist track. Rates include dinner and breakfast. **£££**

Cockermouth

The Allerdale Court Hotel, Market Place, tel: 01900 823654; www.allerdalecourthotel.co.uk Comfortable guest rooms and two restaurants in a 17th-century house. Fletcher Christian is said to have sought refuge here after he returned from the South Pacific. **££**

Coniston

Sun Hotel, tel: 015394 41248; www.thesunconiston.com Mementos of Donald Campbell's Coniston Water speed bids and fine views. Pub adjacent. **££**

Beech Tree Guest House, Yewdale Road, tel: 015394 41717. Guest house with attractive grounds. **£**

Ennerdale Bridge

Shepherd's Arms Hotel, tel: 01946 861249; www.shepherdsarmshotel.co.uk Traditional village inn and award-winning real ale pub. Fine food. **£**

Eskdale

The Brook House Hotel, Boot, tel: 019467 23288. Victorian house by Ravenglass-Eskdale Railway. **£**

Forest How Guest House, Eskdale Green, tel: 019467 23201; www.foresthow-eskdale-cumbria.co.uk Beautiful gardens. Great breakfasts. **£**

Grange-over-Sands

Netherwood Hotel, tel: 015395 32552; www.netherwood-hotel.co.uk Luxury accommodation in a 19th-century house with fine views from the elevated restaurant. **£££**

Greenacres Country Guest House, Lindale, tel: 015395 34578. Attractive cottage at the foot of Winster Valley. Log fire in the lounge. **£**

Grasmere

Lake View Country House, Lake View Drive, tel: 015394 35384; www.lakeview-grasmere.com Overlooking Grasmere Lake. **££**

Ash Cottage, Red Lion Square, tel: 015394 35224; www.ashcottage.com Central location. Garden. **£**

Grizedale

Grizedale Lodge, The Hotel in the Forest, tel: 015394 36532. In the heart of Grizedale Forest, approached from near Hawkshead. Restaurant under personal supervision of proprietors. **££**

Hawkshead

Ivy House Hotel, Main Street, tel: 015394 36204; www.ivyhousehotel.com Family-run hotel. Informal atmosphere. **££**

Borwick Lodge, Outgate, tel: 015394 36332; www.borwicklodge.com Seventeenth-century country house set in landscaped gardens; splendid views. **££**

Red Lion Inn, The Square, tel: 015394 36213. Comfortable 15th-century coaching inn. **££**

Kendal District

Heaves Hotel, Heaves, tel: 015395 60396, www.heaveshotel.co.uk Well-preserved Georgian mansion with large bedrooms, a library and great views. **££**

Garnett House Farm, Burneside, tel: 01539 724542; www.garnetthousefarm.co.uk Dairy/sheep farm. En suite bedrooms **£**

Low Jock Scar Country Guest House, Selside, tel: 01539 823259; email: ljs@avmail.co.uk Riverside gardens and good home cooking. **£**

Keswick District

The Lodore Falls Hotel, near Lodore Falls, Borrowdale, tel: 017687 77285; www.lodorefallshotel.co.uk Luxury hotel with excellent facilities. Some rooms overlook Derwent Water. **£££**

The Mill Inn, Mungrisdale, tel/fax:

*Waterhead Hotel,
Ambleside*

01768 779632. Former mill cottage. Good food. **£££**

The Pheasant, Bassenthwaite Lake, nr Cockermouth, tel: 01768 776234; www.the-pheasant.co.uk This heavily beamed former coaching inn lies in a peaceful setting. **£££**

Aaron Lodge, Brunholme Road, tel: 017687 72399; www.aaronlodge.keswick.co.uk Former stationmaster's house. Five minutes from town centre. **££**

The Anchorage, Ambleside Road, tel: 017687 72813; www.anchorage-keswick.co.uk Small guest house, en suite rooms and good views. Near the lake and park **£**

The Cottage in the Wood, Whinlatter Pass, Braithwaite, tel: 017687 78409; www.thecottageinthewood.co.uk Former coaching inn. **££**

Langdales

Elterwater Park Country Guest House, Skelwith Bridge, tel: 015394 31768; www.elterwater.com Sweeping views. **££**

New Dungeon Ghyll Hotel, Great Langdale, tel: 015394 37213; www.dungeon-ghyll.com With 6 acres (2.5 hectares) of fellside. **££**

Three Shires Inn, Little Langdale, tel: 015394 37215. Nineteenth-century inn. Quiet valley **££**

Newby Bridge nr Ulverston

The Coach House, Hollow Oak, Haverthwaite, tel: 015395 31622; www.coachho.com Small, attractive B&B in converted coach house and stables with wooden beams and many other original features. Pleasant garden. **£**

Ullswater District

Sharrow Bay, Howton, tel: 017684 86301. Luxury hotel in Italianate style, set in formal gardens overlooking Ullswater. Well-known restaurant. **£££**

Glenridding Hotel, tel: 017684

82228; www.glenriddinghotel.co.uk Large hotel. Facilities include indoor swimming pool and sauna. **££**

Netherdene Guest House, Troutbeck, tel: 017684 83475; www.netherdene.co.uk Attractive, comfortable country house set in landscaped gardens. **£**

Ulverston

Lonsdale House Hotel, tel: 01229 582598; www.lonsdalehousehotel.co.uk Good location. Some rooms with four-poster bed and jacuzzi. **££**

> **B&B with the National Trust**
> More than 80 tenants of National Trust properties offer bed and breakfast accommodation. Most are fairly inexpensive and invariably the properites are attractive ones, set in beautiful countryside. Contact the National Trust on: 0870 458 4000 for a copy of their leaflet giving full details, or download a copy from their website: www.nationaltrust.org.uk

Whitehaven

Moresby Hall, Moresby, tel: 01946 696317; www.moresbyhall.co.uk Comfortable, well run, country guesthouse in a 17th-century Grade I listed building just outside of Whitehaven. A good base for exploring the Western Lakes. **££**

Windermere and Bowness

Miller Howe Hotel, Rayrigg Road, tel: 01539 442536; www.millerhowe.com Prestigious luxury hotel with stunning views and fine cuisine. Rates include dinner and breakfast. **£££**

The Fairfield, Brantfell Road, Bowness, tel: 015394 46565; email: tonyandliz@the-fairfield.co.uk Old house surrounded by gardens. **££**

Newstead, New Road, Windermere, tel: 015394 44485, www.newstead-guest-house.co.uk Large Victorian house with many original features. **££**

INDEX

Register with
HotelClub.com
and get *£10!*

At *HotelClub.com*, we reward our Members with discounts and free stays in their favourite hotels. As a Member, every booking made by you through *HotelClub.com* will earn you Member Dollars.

When you register, we will credit your account with *£10* which you can use for your next booking! The equivalent of *£10* will be credited in US$ to your Member account (as *HotelClub Member Dollars*). All you need to do is log on to *www.HotelClub.com/compactguides*. Complete your details, including the Membership Number and Password located on the back of the *HotelClub.com* card.

Over 3.5 million Members already use Member Dollars to pay for all or part of their hotel bookings. Join now and start spending Member Dollars whenever and wherever you want – you are not restricted to specific hotels or dates!

With great savings of up to 60% on over 25,000 hotels across 120 countries, you are sure to find the perfect location for business or pleasure. Happy travels from *HotelClub.com*!

www.insightguides.com

OVER 250 DESTINATIONS IN 14 LANGUAGES

Let us be your guide

Your first visit – or a familiar destination? A short stay – or an extended exploration? Whatever your needs, there's an Insight Guide in a format to suit you. From Alaska to Zanzibar, we'll help you discover your world with great pictures, insightful text, easy-to-use maps, and invaluable advice.